To

_____

From

_____

Message

_____

_____

_____

God's Abundant Love

© Copyright 2003 B.J. Hoff

© 2003 Christian Art Gifts, RSA
        Christian Art Gifts Inc., IL, USA

Designed by Christian Art Gifts

ISBN 1-86920-136-1

Printed in China

04 05 06 07 08 09 10 11 12 13 – 11 10 9 8 7 6 5 4 3 2

GOD'S
ABUNDANT
LOVE

One Minute Devotions

B.J. Hoff

christian
art gifts

January

JANUARY 1

THIS NEW YEAR

Lord, let me welcome the challenge
of this new year,
with hope in my heart
and faith in Your goodness.
Let me look forward to each day on the way
as a many-splendored gift from You.

*Go in peace. Your journey
has the LORD's approval.*

Judges 18:6

JANUARY 2

FATHER GOD

Creator God ... that You,
on whose sovereign will
time itself depends and eternity hinges,
would name me as Your beloved
and bid me call You Father,
is more than I can comprehend ...
I bow before You.

Let the beloved of the
LORD rest secure in him.

Deuteronomy 33:12

JANUARY 3

LIFE IS A GIFT

Life is a gift –
and I celebrate it!
The future is Yours, Lord –
and I welcome it!

Thanks be to God for
his indescribable gift!
2 Corinthians 9:15

JANUARY 4

LOVE, GRACE, MERCY

Thank You for filling my past and my present
with Your love and Your grace and Your mercy.
Thank You for the promise
that I will spend all my tomorrows with You.

*We have this hope as an
anchor for the soul, firm and secure.*
Hebrews 6:19

JANUARY 5

EVERYDAY PURPOSE

Lord, be my daily guide upon the journey.
Help me find Your purpose
for my life in the everyday.
Let me catch a glimpse of Your glory
in the commonplace.
Make me wise enough
to treasure the here and now
as I trust the future to You.

*The LORD himself goes before you and will be
with you; he will never leave you nor forsake you.*

Deuteronomy 31:8

JANUARY 6

GIVE YOU GLORY

Author of my faith,
may every beat of my heart,
every breath of my life,
reach beyond and rise above
the song of self to give You glory.

*Hallelujah! For our Lord God
Almighty reigns. Let us rejoice
and be glad and give him glory!*

Revelation 19:6

JANUARY 7

THIS QUIET MOMENT

I have set apart this quiet moment,
where worldly cares cannot intrude.
I kneel before You in my heart, Lord –
in Your peace I am renewed.

Peace I leave with you; my peace I give
you. I do not give to you as the world gives.
John 14:27

JANUARY 8

EACH NEW DAY

Oh, Lord, how You love to bless us ...
You stand waiting with the dawn
of each new day with a fresh supply
of goodness and gladness and grace
for the hours to come.

His compassions never fail.
They are new every morning.
Lamentations 3:22-23

JANUARY 9

LIGHTING EVERY STEP

Lord, light my every step upon life's journey.
Whether I'm walking or standing still,
changing courses or pressing straight ahead,
may I live every moment
close to You, in Your love.

I am the LORD your God, who
directs you in the way you should go.
Isaiah 48:17

JANUARY 10

DELIGHT IN LIFE

Teach me to delight my heart
in all of life, each precious part.

Rejoice in the Lord always.
I will say it again: Rejoice!
Philippians 4:4

JANUARY 11

LORD OF FOREVER

Lord of my life, my forevers ...
I thank You
for being with me
through all my yesterdays ...
I trust You,
for You hold my tomorrows
in Your hand.

He has made everything beautiful in its time.
Ecclesiastes 3:11

JANUARY 12

IN YOUR HANDS

Your Power is my courage,
Your Promises, my comfort,
Your Presence, my confidence –
I rest my life, my soul, my future
in Your hands.

My times are in your hands.

Psalm 31:15

JANUARY 13

PEACE WITHIN YOUR LOVE

Lord, still the clamor of our days
and calm our rushing anxious ways.
In silence, teach us how to praise –
give us peace within Your love.

Come to me, all you who are weary and
burdened, and I will give you rest.
Matthew 11:28

JANUARY 14

THE SHADOW OF HIS CARE

There is nowhere we can go
that God has not been there before us –
we walk always in the shadow
of His presence and His care.

*When he has brought out all his own, he goes
on ahead of them, and his sheep follow him.*

John 10:4

JANUARY 15

ANOTHER SUNRISE

Our Loving Lord ...
What strength it gives, what peace it lends,
to know that whatever this day may hold,
Your promises stand,
unchanging and unfailing ...
and however this day may end,
Your love will greet another sunrise.

The LORD is faithful to all his promises
and loving toward all he has made.
Psalm 145:13

JANUARY 16

THE LIFETIME OF MY DAYS

He leads me through
the lifetime of my days ...
He teaches me in countless little ways ...
He guides me on so many paths unknown ...
He guards me as a Shepherd keeps His own.

*Your ears will hear a voice behind you,
saying, "This is the way; walk in it."*

Isaiah 30:21

JANUARY 17

THE SHELTER OF YOUR LOVE

Prince of Peace,
in the rush of the world around me
let me stand quietly
in the shelter of Your love.

For he himself is our peace.

Ephesians 2:14

JANUARY 18

TRUE CONTENTMENT

Lord,
grant me true contentment ...
acceptance of what each day brings,
joy in You and not in things.

*I have learned to be content whatever
the circumstances. I can do everything
through him who gives me strength.*

Philippians 4:11, 13

JANUARY 19

In all things

Though I know the world will fail me, Lord,
I know You never will.
You have promised to be with me
in all things.

I am with you always, to
the very end of the age.
Matthew 28:20

JANUARY 20

YOUR MARVELOUS GRACE

Rock of Ages ...
When I am at my weakest point,
You are just beginning.
Lord, I abide in Your marvelous grace;
I lean on Your never-failing love.

My grace is sufficient for you, for
my power is made perfect in weakness.
2 Corinthians 12:9

JANUARY 21

A NEW HORIZON

Lord of eternal sunrise,
help me look past the night,
to view a new horizon
bathed in hope and peace and light.

The LORD is my light and my salvation.

Psalm 27:1

JANUARY 22

GOD HOLDS MY HAND

Secure in the promise
that God holds my hand,
I look to His leading each day.
Assured that He works
through all things for my best,
I follow, I trust, and I pray.

*In your unfailing love you will
lead the people you have redeemed.*

Exodus 15:13

JANUARY 23

SOURCE OF LIFE

When my faith would fail or falter
under the burdens of life,
let me keep my eyes on You, Lord,
the blessed Source of life.

He who has the Son has life.
1 John 5:12

JANUARY 24

MY HAVEN

The shelter of Your love Lord,
is my haven. Freed from the struggle
of trying to fulfill my own dreams
and order my own life,
I can rest in Your arms and be at peace.

God is our refuge and strength,
an ever-present help in trouble.

Psalm 46:1

JANUARY 25

ABIDE IN THEE

Lord, free us from the chains that bind –
the fear that steals our peace of mind,
the worry that disputes Your grace,
the deadly doubt that would replace
our faith and hope ...
Lord, set us free
and teach us to abide in Thee.

Through Christ Jesus the law
of the Spirit of life set me free.

Romans 8:2

JANUARY 26

STRENGTH FOR THE JOURNEY

You are the Way – the one and only Way ...
and I choose to walk with You
on the life-long journey to wholeness ...
and holiness ...
Lord, give me strength for the journey.

Direct me in the path of your commands,
for there I find delight. Turn my
eyes away from worthless things.
Psalm 119:35, 37

JANUARY 27

GOD'S LOVE

Only love ... God's love ... can give
fresh meaning to each day I live.

I have loved you with an everlasting love;
I have drawn you with loving-kindness.

Jeremiah 31:3

JANUARY 28

OUR SHEPHERD

The Shepherd doesn't call His sheep
to unfamiliar pasture –
He has promised that, where we are,
we will also find Him there.

He tends his flock like a shepherd.
Isaiah 40:11

JANUARY 29

MY FAITHFUL GUIDE

Jesus, my faithful pilot and guide ...
help me to begin each new day
with Your name in my thoughts,
Your love in my heart,
Your Spirit at my side to guide and lead me.

*Since we live by the Spirit, let
us keep in step with the Spirit.*
Galatians 5:25

JANUARY 30

BLESSINGS OF BEAUTY

Quiet my heart, Lord;
make me keenly aware
of the blessings of beauty
all around me
and continually grateful
for the confirmation of Your love
in all of life.

He will quiet you with his love.

Zephaniah 3:17

January 31

The first light of morning

Lord, smile down on this new day ...
meet me at the first light of the morning.
Open my eyes and my heart
with an early touch of Your grace
and a fresh new gift of Your love.

*Inwardly we are being
renewed day by day.*
2 Corinthians 4:16

February

FEBRUARY 1

MY HOPE

In fear, You are my Fortress ...
in darkness, You are my Light ...
in doubt, You are my Confidence ...
in despair, You are my Hope ...
in the shelter of Your Love, I am secure.

Keep me safe, O God,
for in you I take refuge.
Psalm 16:1

FEBRUARY 2

TRUST

I trust my todays
and all my tomorrows
to the One who holds
eternity in His hands.

*Surely goodness and love will
follow me all the days of my life.*
Psalm 23:6

FEBRUARY 3

YOUR STEADFAST LOVE

Teach me to wait patiently in the silence ...
to trust Your guiding hand,
Your perfect will, Your steadfast love
even when I'm feeling most alone.

*Your Father knows what you
need before you ask him.*

Matthew 6:8

FEBRUARY 4

GIFTS OF GOODNESS

The landscape of a day
is never barren ...
upon each hour is painted
gifts of goodness and God's grace.

This is the day the LORD has made;
let us rejoice and be glad in it.

Psalm 118:24

FEBRUARY 5

GOD WILL GUIDE

If we search, God will guide.
If we pray, He will hear.
If we need, He will provide.
If we reach, He will draw near.

Everyone who asks receives;
he who seeks finds; and to him who
knocks, the door will be opened.
Luke 11:10

FEBRUARY 6

DESIRES AND DREAMS

May my only ambition always be
to fulfill Your will for my life, Lord ...
Let my desires and my dreams,
my hopes and my plans,
be planted and approved by You.

Am I now trying to win the approval of
men, or of God? If I were still trying to please
men, I would not be a servant of Christ.
Galatians 1:10

FEBRUARY 7

ANSWERED PRAYER

Only the Lord can turn faith to strength,
hope to health,
and the longing of the heart
to answered prayer.

*For in him we live and
move and have our being.*
Acts 17:28

FEBRUARY 8

THE FIRST STEP

Which road to take ... which sign to follow?
Which of the choices before me is best?
Lord, shake the dust from my feet,
give me courage to take the first step,
trusting You for the rest.

*If the LORD delights in a man's
way, he makes his steps firm.*
Psalm 37:23

February 9

Heart of love

Compassionate Savior ...
we cannot hope to comprehend
Your heart of love,
Your well of mercy,
Your continual awareness of our need ...
but we believe and cling to the assurance
that we are Your own,
known and loved and cherished
heart by heart, soul by soul, one by one.

I love those who love me, and
those who seek me find me.

Proverbs 8:17

FEBRUARY 10

AT THE CROSS

Here, Lord, at the cross,
I exchange my pain for peace,
my loss for gain,
my heartache for hope.

*Let us then approach the throne
of grace with confidence, so that
we may receive mercy and find
grace to help us in our time of need.*
Hebrews 4:16

February 11

The forgiving eyes of love

How grateful I am, Lord,
that when You look upon me,
You bypass my imperfect outward appearance
and my even less perfect heart
to see me as Your child,
redeemed by the Cross,
made acceptable by the sacrifice of Your Son ...
Thank You, Lord, for looking at me
through the forgiving eyes of love.

*For he chose us in him before the creation of
the world to be holy and blameless in his sight.*

Ephesians 1:4

FEBRUARY 12

GOD IS GREATER

God is greater than all life's problems,
greater than heartache or pain –
when the world and its trouble
are remembered no more,
God's love will always remain.

In this world you will have trouble. But
take heart! I have overcome the world.
John 16:33

FEBRUARY 13

PROVIDENCE AND PROMISES

Lord, I fear only when I forget
Your providence and Your promises.
Let me live each day mindful
of all You have done for me in the past –
and hopeful of all You will do
in the days to come.

*Be careful that you do not
forget the LORD your God.*

Deuteronomy 8:11

FEBRUARY 14

GIFT OF THE DAY

For every dear, familiar face in my life ...
every smile, every touch, every grace ...
for every gift of the day,
no matter how commonplace it may appear ...
I give You thanks with every breath I take.

I will be joyful in God my Savior.
Habakkuk 3:18

FEBRUARY 15

TRUST AND OBEY

Lord, the only truth is Your truth,
the only wisdom, Your wisdom ...
Let my response to both
be uncompromising honesty
and unquestioning obedience.

If any of you lacks wisdom, he should
ask God, who gives generously to all without
finding fault, and it will be given to him.

James 1:5

FEBRUARY 16

FURNISH MY HEART

With the light of Your presence
and the warmth of Your love, Lord,
furnish my heart ... and make it Your home.

For God made his light shine in
our hearts to give us the light of
the knowledge of the glory of God.

2 Corinthians 4:6

FEBRUARY 17

MY HEART SET ON YOU

Lord, keep my focus on You ...
Let me not be distracted
or diverted from Your will
by ideas or things or even people ...
Keep my eyes, my heart, set on You.

Let us fix our eyes on Jesus, the
author and perfecter of our faith.
Hebrews 12:2

57

FEBRUARY 18

GOD KNOWS BEST

Be content, my heart,
though you cannot see
God's vast eternal mystery.
Be at peace, my soul,
like a child at rest,
in the simple truth
that God knows best.

Be still, and know that I am God.
Psalm 46:10

FEBRUARY 19

QUIET MY HEART

Help me to step back, Lord,
from the noise of the crowd,
the tumult of life's problems,
the clamor and confusion of the world ...
Quiet my heart,
that I may hear Your whisper.

*But the LORD was not in the wind ... not
in the earthquake ... not in the fire.
And after the fire came a gentle whisper.*
1 Kings 19:11-12

FEBRUARY 20

A STRENGTH THAT NEVER FAILS

Lord, You are my hope, my consolation ...
In the gentle warmth of Your love,
there is a strength that never fails,
a fortress and a hiding place
where I need never fear.

*You will be secure, because there
is hope; you will look about
you and take your rest in safety.*

Job 11:18

FEBRUARY 21

A BEACON OF HOPE

Treasure the memories of all God has done
in the past to sustain and restore us ...
Call them to mind like a beacon of hope,
always shining with promise before us.

The LORD appeared to us in the past,
saying: "I have loved you with an
everlasting love; I will build you up again."
Jeremiah 31:3-4

FEBRUARY 22

YOUR MIGHTY ARMS

When I'm convinced
I cannot go another step,
You sweep me into Your mighty arms
and carry me the rest of the way.

The eternal God is your refuge,
and underneath are the everlasting arms.

Deuteronomy 33:27

FEBRUARY 23

CHERISH EVERY MOMENT

Teach me to cherish
every moment of my life ...
to recognize the blessing
and the gift of the here and now,
instead of racing through my days
on the way to the future.

Encourage one another daily,
as long as it is called Today.
Hebrews 3:13

February 24

New blessings

His love greets us every morning
with new blessings for the day ...
With each sunrise we embrace
the grace of God.

*He is like the light of morning
at sunrise on a cloudless morning.*

2 Samuel 23:4

FEBRUARY 25

THE PROMISE OF ETERNITY

When I am tempted
to yearn for what is not,
God brings to my mind
the gentle thought that His will
is more than enough for me ...
For I have been promised eternity.

Rejoice and be glad, because
great is your reward in heaven.
Matthew 5:12

FEBRUARY 26

HOPEFUL THINGS

The Lord will heal my broken wings,
my shattered dreams,
with whole and healthy, hopeful things ...
He restores my wounded soul.

Heal me, O LORD, and I will be
healed; save me and I will be
saved, for you are the one I praise.
Jeremiah 17:14

FEBRUARY 27

ENCOURAGED BY YOUR LOVE

Lord, You have promised me
that Your love never fails,
and time and time again
I have seen that promise fulfilled ...
Through every trial, in every storm,
I am strengthened
and encouraged by Your love.

May your unfailing love be my comfort,
according to your promise to your servant.

Psalm 119:76

FEBRUARY 28

GOD HOLDS ON

When I step out on unknown paths,
it helps me to recall
that I may slip, but God holds on –
He will not let me fall.

*I will strengthen you and help you; I
will uphold you with my righteous right hand.*

Isaiah 41:10

FEBRUARY 29

HERE AND NOW

Lord, my place may not be a royal place,
but You have led me here ...
My task may not be a noble task,
but You have appointed it to me ...
May I fulfil Your purpose
for this moment in my life
by being obedient to Your will
here and now.

*"And who knows but that you have come to
royal position for such a time as this?"*

Esther 4:14

March

MARCH 1

THE TAPESTRY

When I'm tempted to think
that my one small life
makes no difference
in God's plan for eternity,
He gently reminds me
that it takes each unique thread
to complete the design of a tapestry.

*I pray also that the eyes of your heart
may be enlightened in order that you may
know the hope to which he has called
you, the riches of his glorious inheritance.*

Ephesians 1:18

MARCH 2

A TOUCH OF GLORY

Thank You for bringing
a touch of Your glory,
a gift of Your love,
to the small things and
everyday places of my life.

And we, who with unveiled faces all reflect
the Lord's glory, are being transformed into
his likeness with ever-increasing glory.
2 Corinthians 3:18

MARCH 3

NEW HOPES AND ASPIRATIONS

Every morning dawns upon
new hopes and aspirations,
every sunrise brings to us
a chance to start again ...
Every evening lends
its peace and quiet inspiration,
every sunset blesses us
with thoughts of what has been.

There is a time for everything, and
a season for every activity under heaven.
Ecclesiastes 3:1

MARCH 4

A LEGACY OF LOVE

We have been given all things from above,
a legacy gained from a treasury of love,
endowed by a King
who owns heaven and earth,
yet sees us as precious, of infinite worth.

*The Father has qualified you to
share in the inheritance of the
saints in the kingdom of light.*

Colossians 1:12

MARCH 5

A LIFE MADE NEW

You came to me behind the closed doors
of my sin, my doubt, and my confusion ...
I came to You with the gift of
myself – a life made new, a heart
made clean and surrendered ...
For now and forever, I am Yours, Lord.

*But now in Christ Jesus you who
once were far away have been brought
near through the blood of Christ.*

Ephesians 2:13

MARCH 6

A FOREVER FRIEND

Lord, You are faithful and unfailing,
a Forever Friend.
Forgive me for all the times
I've looked elsewhere for security,
founding my hope on people or things,
when in my heart I know,
there is no real refuge but You.

God is love. This is how God showed his love
among us: He sent his one and only Son into
the world that we might live through him.

1 John 4:8-9

MARCH 7

THE LOVE OF CHRIST

Teach us, Lord, to love as You love –
freely, fully, unselfishly, unconditionally.
Fill us with the love of Christ
and make us one in You.

Dear children, let us not love with words
or tongue but with actions and in truth.
1 John 3:18

MARCH 8

LIGHT AND TRUTH

Lord, let me live one day at a time ...
my choices determined by Your will,
my path illumined by Your light,
my faith grounded in Your truth,
my heart set on eternity.

*I guide you in the way of wisdom
and lead you along straight paths.*

Proverbs 4:11

MARCH 9

THE BRANCH OF HOPE

Lord, Your love
is the branch of hope I cling to ...
In the rising tide,
in the restless wind,
in the gathering storm,
You are my peace.

*You will keep in perfect peace him whose
mind is steadfast, because he trusts in you.*

Isaiah 26:3

MARCH 10

A SONG OF HOPE

Lord, give me a dream to cling to,
a song of hope to sing to,
an offering of love to bring to You,
my Savior and my King.

*May the God of hope fill you with all
joy and peace as you trust in him.*

Romans 15:13

MARCH 11

DAY BY DAY

Help me to live day by day,
with the assurance that the Lord
who walked beside me in my yesterdays
is the Lord who will walk beside me
through all my days.

The LORD replied, "My Presence will go
with you, and I will give you rest."
Exodus 33:14

MARCH 12

GOD'S LOVE

God's love goes far beyond our dreams,
beyond our aspirations ...
His love surpasses all our plans,
our hopes and expectations.

*I pray that you may grasp how wide and
long and high and deep is the love of Christ, and
to know this love that surpasses knowledge.*
Ephesians 3:17-19

MARCH 13

STEPPING-STONES

God makes stepping-stones of all our days
to guide us on life's pathway.
When we would stand where we are,
in the safety of this hour,
He bids us move, step out, and follow Him.

I run in the path of your commands,
for you have set my heart free.
Psalm 119:32

MARCH 14

HAND OF LOVE

Let me take nothing for granted, Lord,
especially the small and simple things,
the pure and lovely
but often inconspicuous things ...
Help me to see in all things
Your creative hand of love.

The whole earth is full of his glory.

Isaiah 6:3

MARCH 15

THE SPLENDOR OF BEAUTY

Today, look upon something beautiful ...
For beauty is a gift of God,
a touch of wonder, a glimpse of glory,
a hint of great and splendid things,
eternal things to be.

Every good and perfect gift is from above.
James 1:17

MARCH 16

OPEN MY HEART

Open my hands, Lord ...
Help me to let go
of those worldly treasures
to which I cling.
Open my heart, Lord ...
Help me to make room
for the heavenly treasures
Your Spirit will bring.

*Where your treasure is, there
your heart will be also.*
Matthew 6:21

MARCH 17

SHOWERS OF GOODNESS

Our God delights in
pouring out His blessings,
showering us with goodness every day ...
It pleases God to show us, His beloved,
the wondrous things that happen when we pray.

*And pray in the Spirit on all occasions
with all kinds of prayers and requests.*
Ephesians 6:18

MARCH 18

A QUIET HEART

Give me, Lord, a quiet heart,
a tranquil soul, a peaceful spirit.
No matter how the world may rage around me,
give me a secret place where I may go
and rest in You.

For in the day of trouble he will keep me safe
in his dwelling; he will hide me in the shelter of
his tabernacle and set me high upon a rock.

Psalm 27:5

MARCH 19

FAITH'S RAINBOW

There is a rainbow in the soul
for every storm that comes to us ...
Faith is our assurance
that the sun will shine again.

*Have faith in the LORD your
God and you will be upheld.*
2 Chronicles 20:20

MARCH 20

THE CENTER OF MY LIFE

You are the center of my life, Lord.
Between me and every storm,
every problem, every sorrow,
is Your presence, Your protection
and Your power.

He is a shield to those who take refuge in him.

Proverbs 30:5

MARCH 21

A BEACON ON MY FAITH

Light of the world,
Your love is the sunrise
that makes all my days new.
Your love lights my soul
and shines a beacon on my faith.

God is light; in him there is no darkness at all.

1 John 1:5

MARCH 22

ENDLESS LOVE

Mountains, valleys, land and sea –
all this God shares with you and me;
yet all creation's glorious best
could never measure how we're blessed
by one great gift beyond compare –
our Creator's endless love and care.

Worship him who made the heavens,
the earth, the sea and the springs of water.
Revelation 14:7

MARCH 23

SECURE IN HIS LOVE

The One who made the world, created life,
and prepared eternity,
holds us as a Shepherd carries His lambs ...
in His power, in His love, we are secure.

The LORD is the strength of his people.
Save your people and bless your inheritance;
be their shepherd and carry them forever.
Psalm 28:8-9

MARCH 24

CLOSE TO YOU

I trust You with the details of my days, Lord –
I pray to know Your will,
I praise you for what You send,
I rejoice in the peace of living
close to You.

Be joyful always; pray continually;
give thanks in all circumstances, for this
is God's will for you in Christ Jesus.
1 Thessalonians 5:16-18

MARCH 25

CALVARY

Lamb of God ...
Thank You for standing in for me at Calvary,
for taking my place, erasing my sin,
redeeming my soul.

Worthy is the Lamb, who was slain, to
receive power and wealth and wisdom and
strength and honor and glory and praise!
Revelation 5:12

MARCH 26

I THANK GOD

For the mercy I could never deserve,
the debt I could never repay,
the love I could never earn ...
I thank God every day.

It is by grace you have been
saved, through faith – and this not
from yourselves, it is the gift of God.
Ephesians 2:8

MARCH 27

LASTING GOOD

With God as my guide,
the unknown becomes a challenge ...
There is nothing He cannot redeem
and turn to lasting good.

And we know that in all things God works
for the good of those who love him, who
have been called according to his purpose.
Romans 8:28

MARCH 28

A CONSTANT DELIGHT

Make me a constant delight
to Your heart, Lord.
Let my life always give You
a reason to smile.

He will take great delight in you,
he will quiet you with his love, he
will rejoice over you with singing.

Zephaniah 3:17

MARCH 29

TENDER LOVE

Though the multitude may press Him,
we are blessed that God's own Son
cares for every child as tenderly
as if there were but one.

The LORD watches over all who love him.

Psalm 145:20

MARCH 30

A PLEASING CHILD

Make me, Lord,
a pleasing child to Thee,
a special friend to Thee,
a source of delight to Thee –
make me, Lord,
whatever You want me to be.

Yet you know me, O LORD; you see me
and test my thoughts about you.

Jeremiah 12:3

MARCH 31

QUIET, UNEXPECTED WAYS

God often comes to us,
not in the dramatic and the spectacular,
but in quiet, unexpected ways ...
In a still, small voice, a gentle whisper,
God makes known His love.

In quietness and trust is your strength.

Isaiah 30:15

April

APRIL 1

A PRICELESS GIFT

Anything entrusted to His keeping,
anything turned over to His care,
is changed into a new and precious blessing,
a timeless, priceless gift beyond compare.

*He who was seated on the throne
said, "I am making everything new!"*
Revelation 21:5

APRIL 2

RIGHT WHERE WE ARE

The Savior's death between
two thieves enables us to see
that He comes to us right where we are,
not where we'd like to be.

Then he said, "Jesus, remember me
when you come into your kingdom."
Jesus answered him, "I tell you the truth,
today you will be with me in paradise."
Luke 23:42-43

APRIL 3

HE'S ALWAYS THERE

He's always there ...
to bear the burden, to share the hours,
to strengthen the heart ...
Our Loving Lord, our Faithful Friend,
the One who cares –
He's always there.

*Blessed is he whose help is the God of
Jacob, whose hope is in the LORD his God,
the LORD, who remains faithful forever.*

Psalm 146:5-6

APRIL 4

FAITH

Faith does not expect
to have all questions answered ...
Faith celebrates the search
and rejoices in life's journey.

It is by faith you stand firm.
2 Corinthians 1:24

APRIL 5

BOUNDARIES

I stand in awe of Your power, Lord,
and newly encouraged that You,
who set the boundaries of the sea,
have also set the boundaries of my life ...
the raging waters may roll against me,
but they cannot prevail ...
they may roar,
but they cannot cross the boundaries
established by my God.

I made the sand a boundary for the sea,
an everlasting barrier it cannot cross.

Jeremiah 5:22

APRIL 6

A SONG OF CELEBRATION

Make of my days a song
to delight Your heart ...
Make my life a celebration
of Your love.

The LORD delights in those who fear him,
who put their hope in his unfailing love.

Psalm 147:11

APRIL 7

MY GOAL

In whatever I say,
in all that I do,
let my goal always be
to help others see You.

*Philip found Nathanael and told him,
"We have found the one Moses wrote
about in the Law, and about whom the
prophets also wrote – Jesus of Nazareth."*
John 1:45

APRIL 8

THE HOLLOW OF HIS HAND

He shields me, though I may not always see
the many ways the Lord delivers me ...
He lifts me when I fall and helps me stand –
He holds me in the hollow of His hand.

*He reached down from on
high and took hold of me.*

Psalm 18:16

APRIL 9

IN LIFE'S STORMS

What keeps me from self-pity
in life's storms, and helps me stand
is a faith that keeps me clinging
to the Savior's nail-scarred hand.

He got up and rebuked the wind
and the raging waters; the
storm subsided, and all was calm.
Luke 8:25

APRIL 10

EVERY BLESSING OF GOODNESS

Rich beyond measure,
we daily receive
every blessing of goodness
God's love can conceive.

Blessings crown the head of the righteous.

Proverbs 10:6

APRIL 11

A LOVE THAT OVERWHELMS

Thank You, Lord, for saving me,
in spite of my sin, in spite of myself ...
I praise You for a love
that overcomes and overwhelms.

*But when the kindness and love of
God our Savior appeared, he saved
us, not because of righteous things we
had done, but because of his mercy.*

Titus 3:4-5

APRIL 12

CHRIST'S FORGIVENESS

The crucified Christ who said,
"Father, forgive them,
for they know not what they do,"
is the same Christ
who opens His arms wide
with love and forgiveness for me and you.

*As far as the east is from the west, so far
has he removed our transgressions from us.*

Psalm 103:12

APRIL 13

A GIFT TO BLESS YOU

Make the most of quiet hours,
let your heart be calm and still ...
believe today that God will send a gift
to bless you ... and He will.

The LORD bless you and keep you;
the LORD make his face shine upon
you and be gracious to you; the LORD turn
his face toward you and give you peace.
Numbers 6:23-25

APRIL 14

WALKING IN YOUR LIGHT

Lord, keep me walking in Your light,
following Your truth, obeying Your Word,
not worrying about what I do or what I am
or where I'm going, but desiring only
Your perfect will for my life.

Teach me to do your will, for you are my God;
may your good Spirit lead me on level ground.
Psalm 143:10

APRIL 15

A SMILE AND A PRAYER

A love-filled thought of a friend
makes the heart smile.
A love-filled prayer for a friend
makes the Lord smile.
Lord, remind us to pray for one another.

*In all my prayers for all of
you, I always pray with joy.*
Philippians 1:4

APRIL 16

THE WELL OF MERCY

Lord, Your well of mercy is overflowing,
Your store of blessings, inexhaustible ...
Sunrise to sunrise, season to season,
Your love is unending and boundless.

Praise the LORD. Give thanks to the LORD,
for he is good; his love endures forever.
Psalm 106:1

APRIL 17

LOVE'S TOUCH

Love's touch can change small things
to priceless treasures;
love's touch transfigures all things
to impart a precious gift of joy
time cannot tarnish –
love's touch is God's own touch
upon the heart.

Keep yourselves in God's love.
Jude 21

APRIL 18

THE PROMISE OF JOY

New every morning, God's mercies abound
to bless every hour of the day ...
The promise of joy in God's presence
is always fulfilled
in a wonderful way.

The LORD is my portion;
therefore I will wait for him.

Lamentations 3:24

APRIL 19

REST IN YOU

Hold me close to
Your heart, Faithful Shepherd.
Shelter me in the haven of Your presence.
Help me to rest in You ... and be at peace.

Save your people and bless your inheritance;
be their shepherd and carry them forever.

Psalm 28:9

APRIL 20

A RAINBOW OF PROMISE

Whatever the storms of life may bring,
never lose sight of God's goodness –
He has painted His promise across the sky
in a rainbow declaring His faithfulness.

*Give thanks to the LORD, for he
is good; his love endures forever.*
Psalm 107:1

APRIL 21

THE GIFT OF A DAY

Lord of life ...
this is the gift of a day
which You have made –
I rejoice in it.
May all I think or say or do
throughout each moment of the day
be rooted in and nourished
by Your love.

The LORD will guide you always;
he will satisfy your needs.
Isaiah 58:11

APRIL 22

THE DEPTH OF HIS LOVE

If the Creator, Lord, and King
of heaven and earth
answers my feeble pleas for help
and shares with me
His eternal truth and wisdom,
why would I ever doubt
the depth of His love
and faithful presence in my life?

This is what the LORD says, he who made the earth,
'Call to me and I will answer you and tell you
great and unsearchable things you do not know.'
Jeremiah 33:3

APRIL 23

THE ACT OF GIVING

Lord, help me to ask less
and give more ...
Let me see the act of giving
as a way to let You love through me.

*See that you also excel
in this grace of giving.*
2 Corinthians 8:7

APRIL 24

THE JOY OF YOUR PRESENCE

Lord, I dedicate this still, quiet time
of the early morning to You ...
In the hush and peace of these silent hours,
I seek nothing more
than to bask in the joy of Your presence.

*Very early in the morning, while it
was still dark, Jesus got up, left
the house and went off to a
solitary place, where he prayed.*
Mark 1:35

APRIL 25

A SURRENDERED HEART

We find God more readily
in the silence of a surrendered heart
than in the whirlwind of a busy world.

The LORD was not in the wind.
The LORD was not in the earthquake.
The LORD was not in the fire.
And after the fire came a gentle whisper.
1 Kings 19:11-12

APRIL 26

A TREASURY OF HOPE

Search out God's promises,
make them a part
Of a treasury of hope
Carefully stored in your heart.

I have hidden your word in my heart.

Psalm 119:11

APRIL 27

PART OF THE MIRACLE

Think of a rainbow,
and storm clouds won't hide
the afternoon sun from your view.
Think of a rose,
and you won't mind the thorns –
they're a part of the miracle, too.

Whatever is true, whatever is noble, whatever
is right, whatever is pure, whatever is lovely,
whatever is admirable – if anything is excellent
or praiseworthy – think about such things.

Philippians 4:8

133

APRIL 28

THE JOY OF YOUR PRESENCE

Day after day, Lord,
year after year
the joy of Your presence
grows even more dear.

Though you have not seen him, you
love him; and even though you do not
see him now, you believe in him and are filled
with an inexpressible and glorious joy.

1 Peter 1:8

APRIL 29

THE BLESSING OF TODAY

Let us live in the blessing of Today ...
Cherishing our memories,
but not holding them too tightly ...
Treasuring our dreams,
but not building our future on them.
Let us live in the present, rejoicing in the gifts
God lends to every moment of Today.

I know that there is nothing better for men
than to be happy and do good while they live.
That everyone may eat and drink, and find
satisfaction in all his toil – this is the gift of God.
Ecclesiastes 3:12-13

APRIL 30

THE HOPE OF HEAVEN

Let me hold the hope of heaven
in my heart throughout life's journey ...
Let me keep my hand in Yours, Lord,
as I travel on the way.

There is surely a future hope for you.
Proverbs 23:18

May

MAY 1

A WONDERFUL WAY

God has provided a wonderful way
for handling life's problems –
just trust Him and pray ...
And when things look brighter
and joy fills our days,
remember to thank Him
by singing His praise.

Is any one of you in trouble?
He should pray. Is anyone happy?
Let him sing songs of praise.
James 5:13

MAY 2

A GLAD HEART

Lord, give me the gift
of a glad heart today
and a faith that lets nothing
stand in the way of Your peace ...
let me trust in Your goodness
and rest in the confidence
Your love will send only my best.

We know that in all things God works
for the good of those who love him.

Romans 8:28

MAY 3

HIS HEALING LOVE

God hears the voice of millions,
each cry unique and special.
Every heart that comes
seeking His healing love
is welcomed and touched
and made whole.

I will bring health and healing to it;
I will heal my people and will let them
enjoy abundant peace and security.

Jeremiah 33:6

MAY 4

SEASON OF SINGING

For sunshine and springtime,
our season of singing –
for Your glories displayed –
thank You, Lord.

*See! The winter is past; the rains are
over and gone. Flowers appear on the
earth; the season of singing has come.*

Song of Solomon 2:11-12

May 5

Abiding in His peace

Strength is often found within the silence,
While resting in the presence of the Lord.
Abiding in His peace, we feel His power;
While leaning on His love, we are restored.

Not by might nor by power, but by
my Spirit, says the Lord Almighty.
Zechariah 4:6

MAY 6

BEYOND OUR DREAMS

His love goes far beyond our dreams,
beyond our aspirations ...
His love surpasses all our plans,
our hopes and expectations.

As the Father has loved me, so have
I loved you. Now remain in my love.
John 15:9

May 7

Beside me

When I think I'm on my own,
He stands beside me.
When I'm feeling most alone,
He comes to guide me.

Be strong and courageous. Do not
be terrified; do not be discouraged,
*for the L*ord *your God will be*
with you wherever you go.

Joshua 1:9

MAY 8

THE LIGHT OF JESUS' LOVE

At the cross of Calvary
I leave the darkness of my soul
and walk away, led by the light
of Jesus' love, renewed and whole.

For you were once darkness,
but now you are light in the
Lord. Live as children of light.

Ephesians 5:8

MAY 9

PRECIOUS JOYS

Morning by morning,
new beauty arrives,
warming our world
as it blesses our lives.
Day after day,
the Lord sends us a treasure
of new joys, too priceless,
too precious to measure.

In the morning, O LORD, you hear my
voice; in the morning I lay my requests
before you and wait in expectation.

Psalm 5:3

MAY 10

RIGHT THERE

How many times, Lord, have I longed
for the peace of Your presence,
the light of Your wisdom,
the comfort of Your love,
when all the while You've been right there,
patiently waiting for me
to come away from the crowd
and commune with You?

Come with me by yourselves to
a quiet place and get some rest.

Mark 6:31

MAY 11

YOUR VISION

Take me as high as You want me to go, Lord,
make me whatever you want me to be.
Lift me above my own narrow horizon
that I might fulfill Your true vision for me.

Those who hope in the LORD will renew their
strength. They will soar on wings like eagles.

Isaiah 40:31

MAY 12

A RAINBOW OF HOPE

Lord, let me carry a rainbow of hope
to the victims of life's storms ...
make my life a bridge
from Your caring heart to the world.

I have set my rainbow in the clouds,
and it will be the sign of the
covenant between me and the earth.

Genesis 9:13

MAY 13

THE HAVEN OF YOUR GRACE

In the harbor of Your peace,
in the haven of Your grace,
in the hollow of Your hand,
I rest my soul.

*I will not forget you! See, I have
engraved you on the palms of my hands.*

Isaiah 49:15-16

MAY 14

MANY WAYS

He comes to us in many ways,
often in unexpected ways ...
Lord, let us never fail to recognize
those things that are of You.

He was in the world, and though
the world was made through him,
the world did not recognize him.

John 1:10

MAY 15

BELOVED

For love of you,
the Savior hung upon a cross.
You are unique.
Beloved.
Never alone.

God did not send his Son into the
world to condemn the world, but
to save the world through him.

John 3:17

MAY 16

YOUR VOICE OF TRUTH

Today, Lord, and every day,
I will set my heart in Your direction,
taking time to be still before You,
to go deeper into Your Word,
to listen carefully for Your voice
of truth and guidance.

Apply your heart to instruction and
your ears to words of knowledge.
Proverbs 23:12

MAY 17

GOD'S GREAT LOVE

So great is Your power, Lord,
that You made us from the dust of the earth ...
So great is Your love, Lord,
that You gave us dominion over Your earth ...
with humble, thankful hearts, we praise You.

*What is man that you are mindful of him, the son of
man that you care for him? You made him a little
lower than the heavenly beings and crowned him with
glory and honor. You made him ruler over the works
of your hands; you put everything under his feet.*

Psalm 8:4-6

MAY 18

THE CROSS OF CALVARY

On the cross, His heart embraced the world,
His death set sinners free ...
God's plan was fulfilled, His love revealed,
on the cross of Calvary.

*Christ loved us and gave himself up for us
as a fragrant offering and sacrifice to God.*

Ephesians 5:2

May 19

For You

Lord, let me live my life for You
seeking Your presence,
trusting Your promises,
singing Your praise every day.

*Teach me your ways so I may know you
and continue to find favor with you.*

Exodus 33:13

MAY 20

FAITHFUL IN ALL THINGS

We can take Him at His word
because the One behind the Word
has proved Himself faithful in all things,
even unto His death upon a cross.

God is not a man, that he should lie,
nor a son of man, that he should
change his mind. Does he speak and then
not act? Does he promise and not fulfill?
Numbers 23:19

MAY 21

A SONG OF PRAISE

Thank You for these mountaintop moments
when my spirit soars and my heart sings.
Thank You for the love that gives my soul
a song of praise.

The LORD is my strength and my shield; my heart
trusts in him, and I am helped. My heart leaps
for joy and I will give thanks to him in song.

Psalm 28:7

MAY 22

FAITH IN YOU

I pray for a faith that will rejoice
as much in the shadows as in the sunshine,
as much in Your promises as in Your gifts,
a faith founded not on what You do –
but simply on YOU.

Anyone who comes to him must
believe that he exists and that he
rewards those who earnestly seek him.
Hebrews 11:6

MAY 23

THE GIFT OF GOD'S LOVE

God's love –
overwhelming, overcoming,
undemanding, understanding ...
God's love –
a gift that cannot be explained,
only received.

Thanks be to God for his indescribable gift!
2 Corinthians 9:15

MAY 24

PATIENT IN HOPE

God wants us to be expectant before Him ...
to wait patiently, but with hope,
to work diligently, but with the understanding
that to Him belong the final results
of all our efforts.

Be still before the LORD
and wait patiently for him.
Psalm 37:7

MAY 25

QUIET BEAUTY

I think God must love best
the simple things, their quiet beauty,
the gentle ordinary things we often do not see.
I think God must be pleased
when we take time to notice small things,
for all things He created
hold a touch of majesty.

By him all things were created: things
in heaven and on earth, visible and invisible.

Colossians 1:16

MAY 26

PEACE AND JOY

What peace – knowing my todays and
my tomorrows rest safely in Your hand ...
What joy – knowing the Creator of the universe
weaves the tapestry of my life.

*He determined the times set for them and
the exact places where they should live.*
Acts 17:26

MAY 27

VICTORY

Lord, turn my trials to triumph,
my times of testing to victory ...
Let me know the blessing
of standing firm for You.

He who stands firm to the end will be saved.

Mark 13:13

MAY 28

A STEADFAST FAITH

Give me, Lord, a steadfast faith
that stands on Your Word
and trusts in Your goodness,
knowing there is never a moment
when I'm out of Your care.

You will keep in perfect peace him whose
mind is steadfast, because he trusts in you.
Isaiah 26:3

MAY 29

A BLESSED HOUR

God can make a blessing of a quiet hour;
His love can turn it into something rare ...
He, and He alone, can make a gift
of precious worth
from anything entrusted to His care.

For you are God my Savior, and
my hope is in you all day long.
Psalm 25:5

MAY 30

QUIET GUIDANCE

Teach me, Lord, to listen
for Your quiet word of guidance ...
Above life's noise and clamor,
let me clearly hear Your voice.

*Those who are led by the
Spirit of God are sons of God.*
Romans 8:14

May 31

Peace, my soul

Peace, my soul, for God is near ...
In the midst of doubt or fear,
I can look beyond and see
His guiding hand reach out to me.

Now may the Lord of peace himself
give you peace at all times and in every
way. The Lord be with all of you.
2 Thessalonians 3:16

June

JUNE 1

CONSTANT REFUGE

God's love stands between us and the storm,
goes before us to unknown places,
guards us from the darkness,
shields us from evil,
holds us to His heart in constant refuge.

*God is our refuge and strength, an ever-present
help in trouble. Therefore we will not fear, though
the earth give way and the mountains fall into the
heart of the sea, though its waters roar and foam
and the mountains quake with their surging.*

Psalm 46:1-3

JUNE 2

EVERYDAY GIFTS OF SPLENDOR

Loving Creator, Thank You
for the everyday gifts of splendor
we so often take for granted.
Remind us to open our eyes
and see Your divine touch
in all things around us.

For you make me glad by your deeds, O LORD;
I sing for joy at the works of your hands.

Psalm 92:4

JUNE 3

AN UNFAILING LIGHT

He's the comforting presence
   we seek in the night.
In life's darkest hour,
He's an unfailing light.

*Let the light of your face
shine upon us, O LORD.*
Psalm 4:6

June 4

His name

Let us rejoice in the beauty
and the power of His name –
Jesus ...
Savior ...
Lord ...

*The name of the LORD is a strong
tower; the righteous run to it and are safe.*

Proverbs 18:10

JUNE 5

FREELY GIVE

When I think of all You've done for me,
can I do less than tell the world
how much You long to do for them?

I have had God's help to this very
day, and so I stand here and
testify to small and great alike.
Acts 26:22

JUNE 6

SECURE IN YOUR LOVE

Gentle Shepherd,
Let me dwell in Your safe pasture,
relying on Your guidance,
abiding in Your presence,
secure within Your love.

*The LORD is my shepherd, I shall
not be in want. He makes me lie
down in green pastures, he leads me
beside quiet waters, he restores my soul.*

Psalm 23:1-3

JUNE 7

HOPES AND DREAMS

I bring to You
my hopes, my plans, my dreams,
for Your safekeeping,
trusting You to do with them
whatever You think best.

Commit your way to the LORD; trust
in him and he will do this: He will make
your righteousness shine like the dawn, the
justice of your cause like the noonday sun.

Psalm 37:5-6

JUNE 8

GOD'S WORD, WILL AND WAY

Believing God's Word,
Seeking God's Will,
Walking God's Way –
This is life lived to the fullest.

Blessed is she who has believed
that what the Lord has said
to her will be accomplished!
Luke 1:45

JUNE 9

GOD'S SILENCE

Even in the quiet, God is working –
His silence in the shadows
does not mean He doesn't care.
A part of faith is trusting without reason,
Believing, when He can't be seen or heard,
That He's still there.

Hope that is seen is no hope at all.
If we hope for what we do not
yet have, we wait for it patiently.
Romans 8:24-25

JUNE 10

THE RAINBOW OF GOD'S LOVE

Look up ...
There glows the rainbow
As the storm fades from our view.
Look up ...
In every storm of life,
God's love is there for you.

A righteous man may have many troubles,
but the LORD delivers him from them all.

Psalm 34:19

June 11

Debt of Love

Oh, Holy God ...
Help me to approach Your throne
with true humility,
ever mindful of the grace
I never earned,
continually thankful for the mercy
I don't deserve
and the awesome debt of love
I can never repay.

Let us be thankful, and so worship
God acceptably with reverence and awe.
Hebrews 12:28

JUNE 12

QUIET DAYS

Thank You, Lord, for the quiet days,
the simple, ordinary days –
even for the difficult days,
when time and time again You prove
that Your faithfulness is unfailing
and Your love is for always.

God has said, "Never will I leave
you; never will I forsake you."
Hebrews 13:5

JUNE 13

FREE TO RUN

You have carried me places
I never could go –
You have given my spirit wings.
You have set me free to run and fly
and reach for heavenly things.

The Sovereign LORD is my strength;
he makes my feet like the feet of a deer,
he enables me to go on the heights.
Habakkuk 3:19

JUNE 14

BEYOND MEASURE

Like a great and mighty river, is the Spirit,
flowing through God's people who believe.
His power is ours in fullness beyond measure,
continually pouring out as we receive.

Whoever believes in me, as
the Scripture has said, streams of
living water will flow from within him.
John 7:38

JUNE 15

LIMITLESS LOVE

His love outreaches time and place
and spans all generations.
His love outgives the greatest gifts –
it knows no limitations.

God is love.
1 John 4:16

JUNE 16

A CHILD TO CHERISH

To God, your life has meaning.
You're someone special –
a child to cherish,
to nurture and to guide.
You belong to God the Father ...
and He loves you.

*Know that the L*ORD *is God. It is*
he who made us, and we are his.

Psalm 100:3

JUNE 17

THE SHELTER OF LOVE

He's a Friend to the lonely,
A safe hiding place ...
We can always find shelter
In God's loving embrace.

He who dwells in the shelter of the Most High
will rest in the shadow of the Almighty.

Psalm 91:1

JUNE 18

LIFE'S JOURNEY

Life's journey includes detours –
changed plans, failed dreams,
wrong-way turns, even dead-ends.
But in His time ... just in time ...
God steps in to give us
wisdom and direction.

He will teach us his ways, so
that we may walk in his paths.
Micah 4:2

JUNE 19

TRUST IN THE PROMISE

When doubt would defeat you,
trust and be still in the promise you're
given while God works His will.

*Our light and momentary troubles
are achieving for us an eternal
glory that far outweighs them all.*

2 Corinthians 4:17

191

JUNE 20

THE STRENGTH OF HUMILITY

Lord, give us more men who can see
the strength to be found in humility,
who understand it is no weakness to be gentle,
who are brave enough
to give their lives away for You.

He is like a tree planted by streams of water,
which yields its fruit in season and whose leaf
does not wither. Whatever he does prospers.

Psalm 1:3

JUNE 21

PERFECT PEACE

I wait on You in perfect peace,
my faith securely anchored,
my soul rejoicing in Your love,
my anxious heart at rest.

*We wait for the blessed hope –
the glorious appearing of our
great God and Savior, Jesus Christ.*

Titus 2:13

JUNE 22

HOPE AND MERCY

We need never run out of hope ...
because God never runs out of mercy.

*Because of his great love for us, God, who
is rich in mercy, made us alive with Christ.*

Ephesians 2:4-5

June 23

Jesus

Jesus, and only Jesus,
is the answer to our every prayer.
He is the Fulfillment ... the Blessing ...
the Solution ... the Healing ...
the Peace that passes all understanding.
Jesus will always be all we need.

Then Jesus declared, "I am the bread of life.
He who comes to me will never go hungry, and
he who believes in me will never be thirsty."
John 6:35

JUNE 24

GOD'S STREAM OF MERCY

Life's struggles won't impede
God's stream of mercy
if we trust His love to always make a way.
And His Spirit will flow out from us to others
if we keep our eyes on Jesus day by day.

Blessed are those who keep my ways.

Proverbs 8:32

JUNE 25

THE MERCIFUL SAVIOR

He is the Lord of Compassion,
who weeps with us, sharing our loss.
He is the merciful Savior,
who purchased our Peace on the Cross.

When he saw the crowds, he had
compassion on them, because they
were harassed and helpless,
like sheep without a shepherd.
Matthew 9:36

JUNE 26

FAITHFUL FRIEND

Faithful Comforter and Friend ...
I thank You for the assurance
of Your presence,
the solace to be found
in just abiding in Your love
and blessed peace.

*You have made known to me the path
of life; you will fill me with joy in
your presence, with eternal
pleasures at your right hand.*

Psalm 16:11

June 27

Fertile Land

There is no place in which I stand
that will not serve as fertile land
for serving my Lord faithfully
as He works out His will through me.

Work out your salvation with fear and
trembling, for it is God who works in you to
will and to act according to his good purpose.
Philippians 2:12-13

199

JUNE 28

SUNSHINE BLESSINGS

Gather from each day
God's sunshine blessings to the heart –
Gentle gifts of beauty, just for you ...
Hold them in your memory,
wrap them carefully with love,
and they will shine with joy forever new.

Rejoice in the LORD and be glad, you righteous;
sing, all you who are upright in heart!

Psalm 32:11

JUNE 29

HIS FATHER'S HEART

God stands with open arms
and outstretched hands
to welcome us home
from wherever we've been,
forgiving our sin,
His Father's heart
rejoicing in our return.

*His father saw him and was filled
with compassion for him; he ran to his son,
threw his arms around him and kissed him.*

Luke 15:20

JUNE 30

GENTLE TIMES

I thank You for the quiet times,
the blessed, peaceful, healing times
in which I can do nothing but rest in You ...
I praise You for the gentle times,
the warm and silent, tranquil times
in which I lean entirely on Your love.

May your unfailing love rest upon us,
O LORD, even as we put our hope in you.
Psalm 33:22

July

JULY 1

COMFORT AND STRENGTH

My comfort and my strength,
as I wait upon Your peace,
is knowing that You are
in this moment with me,
leading me and loving me
through it all.

*I call on the LORD in my
distress, and he answers me.*
Psalm 120:1

JULY 2

THE FAITHFUL SHEPHERD

God will never forsake you,
Nor leave you alone,
For the Shepherd is faithful
To care for His own.

Surely I am with you always,
to the very end of the age.
Matthew 28:20

JULY 3

LIFE-CHANGING LOVE

Lord, let me do my part
in taking Your truth to the world.
Help me start where I am
and do what I can
to communicate
Your life-changing love.

*All over the world this gospel
is bearing fruit and growing.*
Colossians 1:6

JULY 4

LIFE'S MYSTERIES

Leave to God life's mysteries –
all things are in His hands ...
Live each day with childlike faith
as God fulfills His plans.

*I trust in you, O LORD; I say, "You are
my God." My times are in your hands.*
Psalm 31:14-15

JULY 5

FOCUSED FAITH

When we set aside a morning hour
to seek His presence,
our faith is newly focused
on His purpose for our day.

In the morning, O LORD, you hear my
voice; in the morning I lay my requests
before you and wait in expectation.

Psalm 5:3

JULY 6

LOVE OTHERS

How can I thank You
for loving me, Lord,
except to love others
in Your name.

And this is his command: to believe in
the name of his Son, Jesus Christ, and
to love one another as he commanded us.

1 John 3:23

July 7

Closer to Your throne

Lord, let me never forget
that in all things You send, there is blessing ...
Every problem leading me to pray
also leads me deeper into Your presence,
and every trial that takes me to my knees
also brings me closer to Your throne.

Come near to God and he
will come near to you.

James 4:8

JULY 8

A LOVING FATHER

He doesn't wait for us to come
and meet Him at His royal throne –
He comes to us as a loving Father,
reaching out to seek His own.

*For the Son of Man came to
seek and to save what was lost.*
Luke 19:10

JULY 9

MY REFUGE

Oh, Lord, You are my refuge ...
You stand firm and unchanging
with Your Word to give me strength,
Your presence to give me comfort,
Your love to give me hope
and make me whole.

You are my hiding place; you
will protect me from trouble and
surround me with songs of deliverance.

Psalm 32:7

JULY 10

THE COMFORT OF COMPANIONSHIP

When loneliness would darken my heart,
God casts aside the gloom to make room
for the comfort of His companionship
and the soothing light of His love.

God, who has called you into
fellowship with his Son Jesus
Christ our Lord, is faithful.

1 Corinthians 1:9

July 11

Lord and Savior

I cannot separate God's commandments
from His love.
If He is my Savior, He is also my Lord ...
it's an all-or-nothing choice
that includes obedience as well as blessing.

*If anyone loves me, he will obey my
teaching. My Father will love him, and we will
come to him and make our home with him.*

John 14:23

JULY 12

YOU WALK WITH ME

Thank You for the promise
that You hold all my tomorrows
securely in Your hand
as You walk with me on the way.

*Your kingdom is an everlasting kingdom, and your
dominion endures through all generations.*

Psalm 145:13

JULY 13

CHILDREN OF HIS HEART

How many are the promises
that God has given us,
How great the confidence
with which we're blessed:
That we are His beloved,
cherished children of His heart,
Inheritors of all our Father's best.

*In his great mercy he has given us new birth
into a living hope through the resurrection
of Jesus Christ from the dead, and into an
inheritance that can never perish, spoil or fade.*

1 Peter 1:3-4

JULY 14

WE CAN REST

We can rest within God's care –
He doesn't slumber ...
We can wait, for all His promises are true.
We can count on His safekeeping –
He's our Shepherd ...
And what the Lord has promised,
He will do.

*The LORD will keep you from all
harm – he will watch over your life.*

Psalm 121:7

JULY 15

TO GLORIFY YOU

Lord, let me live my life in such a way
that You are glorified every day.
Let my words, my work – whatever I do –
create in others a desire to know You.

*When they saw the courage of Peter and
John and realized that they were unschooled,
ordinary men, they were astonished and they
took note that these men had been with Jesus.*

Acts 4:13

JULY 16

JOY FROM EVERY GIFT

Peace and warm contentment
flow from beauty to the heart –
When God sends quiet
moments, wait and rest ...
Look closely at the lovely things
surrounding you each day,
and take joy from every gift
with which you're blessed.

*"Give thanks to the LORD Almighty, for
the LORD is good; his love endures forever."*

Jeremiah 33:11

JULY 17

THE GLORY OF TODAY

Lord, I want to thank You
for this present hour of blessing,
for the splendor in this shining gift –
the glory of Today.

This is the day the LORD has made;
let us rejoice and be glad in it.
Psalm 118:24

July 18

Blessings of Forgiveness

Lord, make me quick to forgive,
eager to make peace,
forgetful of any wrong committed against me ...
for in every act of forgiveness,
I'm again blessed by Your grace
and the remembrance of all
You've done for me.

*Bear with each other and forgive whatever
grievances you may have against one
another. Forgive as the Lord forgave you.*

Colossians 3:13

JULY 19

A HOPEFUL HEART

Lord, teach me to pray with a hopeful heart,
a heart that expects to be blessed ...
For I know all things that come from Your hand
are good ... and meant for my best.

*He did not waver through unbelief regarding the
promise of God, but was strengthened in his faith
and gave glory to God, being fully persuaded that
God had power to do what he had promised.*

Romans 4:20-21

JULY 20

THINK OF YOUR BLESSINGS

Think of the mountains,
and soon every valley you pass through
will seem very small ...
Think of your blessings,
and soon you'll have no time
to dwell on your problems at all.

Stop and consider God's wonders.
Job 37:14

JULY 21

LIFE ABUNDANT

The Father wants to give us life abundant,
overflowing joy in every hour.
His love for us is steadfast and enduring,
His promises as endless as His power.

And God is able to make
all grace abound to you.
2 Corinthians 9:8

JULY 22

I BELONG TO YOU

Bless me, Lord,
with the peace that comes from knowing
I don't have to struggle to reach You,
I don't have to succeed to please you,
I don't have to do anything
but belong to You and accept
the love and peace You come to bring.

It is for freedom that Christ has set us free.
Stand firm, then, and do not let yourselves
be burdened again by a yoke of slavery.

Galatians 5:1

JULY 23

ETERNAL PROMISES

Let me build my house of life
upon eternal promises:
the Word of God which will not fail
in storm or discontent.

Unless the LORD builds the house,
its builders labor in vain.

Psalm 127:1

JULY 24

GENTLE BLESSINGS

Quiet days are like the sunshine
on a smooth and tranquil sea,
bringing beauty, gentle blessings,
and a still serenity.

The fruit of righteousness will be
peace; the effect of righteousness will
be quietness and confidence forever.
Isaiah 32:17

JULY 25

YOUR INFINITE CARE

Thank You for planning my life, Lord ...
For Your infinite care
with every detail of my days
and the love that designed them all.

All the days ordained for me were written in
your book before one of them came to be.
Psalm 139:16

JULY 26

THE PROMISE OF DAYBREAK

Open your heart to the promise of daybreak;
Welcome each morning, embrace all it brings.
See every dawn as the Father's own promise,
For life is a gift, and it holds wondrous things.

There will be showers of blessing.

Ezekiel 34:26

JULY 27

THE HAVEN OF MY HEART

In every storm, He is unshakeable,
In every struggle, He is steadfast.
In every season of sorrow,
He is the haven of my heart.
In the shelter of His love, I will abide.

*The LORD is my rock, my fortress
and my deliverer; my God is my
rock, in whom I take refuge.*
2 Samuel 22:2-3

JULY 28

SURPRISE VISITS

Lord, let me walk so close to You each day,
that I am always ready with welcome
for Your surprise visits to my life.

*Guide me in your truth and teach
me, for you are God my Savior,
and my hope is in you all day long.*

Psalm 25:5

JULY 29

NEVER FAILING CARE

Ever mindful of His providence,
His never failing care for us,
we celebrate the greatness
and the goodness of our God.

*I will proclaim the name of the L*ORD*. Oh, praise*
the greatness of our God! He is the Rock,
his works are perfect, and all his ways are just.

Deuteronomy 32:3-4

JULY 30

YOU WILL LISTEN

Thank You for the confidence
You have given, Lord,
that I can tell you what's in my heart
and know You will listen,
that I can listen with an open heart
and know You will speak.

Speak, LORD, for your servant is listening.
1 Samuel 3:9

JULY 31

ETERNAL GOD

I'm thankful that my life
was planned and fashioned
by a God of no beginning and no end,
a God to whom a lifetime is a brief touch,
no more than one soft whisper on the wind.

*He chose us in him before the creation of the
world to be holy and blameless in his sight.*

Ephesians 1:4

August

August 1

Peace, be still

Teach me to wait on You, Lord,
to be quiet and wait on Your will ...
Teach me the blessing that comes when I learn
the true meaning of "Peace, be still."

*Perseverance must finish its work so that you may
be mature and complete, not lacking anything.*

James 1:4

AUGUST 2

A SONG OF MY HEART

Thank You for those times, Lord,
when You lead me to the mountain to rejoice ...
Those times You give my heart a song,
my happiness a voice.

I will rejoice in the LORD, I will
be joyful in God my Savior.
Habakkuk 3:18

AUGUST 3

HE IS ABLE

It is not what I can do,
but what *HE* can do ...
not what I can do for *HIM*,
but what *HE* can do through me ...
I am not able ... but *HE* is.

Now to him who is able to do immeasurably
more than all we ask or imagine, according to
his power that is at work within us, to him be
glory in the church and in Christ Jesus throughout
all generations, for ever and ever! Amen.
Ephesians 3:20-21

AUGUST 4

YOUR GUIDING HAND

How thankful I am, Lord,
that You walked with me
through all my yesterdays,
and You will lead me
by Your guiding hand
through all my tomorrows.

If I rise on the wings of the dawn,
if I settle on the far side of the sea,
even there your hand will guide me.
Psalm 139:9-10

AUGUST 5

A GLIMPSE OF HOPE

In our cry for comfort ...
In our need for communion ...
In our search for peace
and a glimpse of hope ...
God is there.
With a Father's heart
and a Father's love,
God is there.

How gracious he will be when you cry for
help! As soon as he hears, he will answer you.

Isaiah 30:19

AUGUST 6

ABIDING JOY

Abiding joy does not depend
upon what's happening around us ...
It exists because of the One
who's living in us.

*The LORD your God will bless you,
and your joy will be complete.*

Deuteronomy 16:15

AUGUST 7

KNOWING YOU

Lord, let me never forget
the excitement and joy
of that moment when I first realized
You loved me ...
Every day, let my life
reflect the light of knowing You.

I saw the Lord.

Isaiah 6:1

August 8

The road through life

One thing the years teach us clearly,
Lord – Your Word ... Your way ... Your will ...
pave the only safe, straight road through life.
Every detour we take around Your wisdom
eventually leads to nowhere.

In all your ways acknowledge him,
and he will make your paths straight.

Proverbs 3:6

August 9

Healing Love

He breaks through all our old ideas
of where to seek His dwelling place
and comes directly to our hearts
with healing love and saving grace.

Seek the LORD and live.
Amos 5:6

AUGUST 10

THE PURPOSE FOR MY DAYS

Keep me close, Lord, help me find
the purpose which Your love designed
for all my days, till this life ends
and Everlasting Life begins.

He has made everything beautiful in its time.
He has also set eternity in the hearts of men.

Ecclesiastes 3:11

AUGUST 11

WAITING IN FAITH

His is the power to guide
and provide for us –
our part is simply to rest,
loving Him, trusting Him,
waiting in faith on Him –
knowing He works for our best.

*Wait for the LORD; be strong and
take heart and wait for the LORD.*
Psalm 27:14

AUGUST 12

A JOUNAL OF HOPE

The heart records the memories
of God's working in our life.
Every account of deliverance
or faith confirmed,
every record of the countless times
God came to rescue,
to comfort, to strengthen or guide
becomes a page in our journal of hope.

*Because of the LORD's great love we are not
consumed, for his compassions never fail.*
Lamentations 3:22

AUGUST 13

BRIGHT HOPE

Begin each day
with your eyes on the rainbow –
Seek the bright hope
and the joy on the way ...
Open your arms wide
and welcome each moment,
gratefully gather the gifts in each day.

There is surely a future hope for
you, and your hope will not be cut off.
Proverbs 23:18

AUGUST 14

SPRINGTIME OF THE SOUL

Summer flowers
will vanish from the garden,
Autumn leaves will fall,
blown by the wind,
Winter's cold will come
and may seem endless ...
But the Springtime of the soul
will never end.

*God has given us eternal life,
and this life is in his Son.*

1 John 5:11

AUGUST 15

A STEADFAST SONG OF PRAISE

In the valley of the shadow
or beside still waters ...
in the depths of despair
or on the heights of joy ...
help me cling to You, Lord,
with a steadfast song of praise.

*Those who know your name will
trust in you, for you, LORD, have
never forsaken those who seek you.*

Psalm 9:10

AUGUST 16

LOVE COMES GENTLY

There are times when shadows fall
and darkness seems to hide Your light.
But then Your love comes gently,
like a star upon the night.

*You are my lamp, O LORD; the
LORD turns my darkness into light.*

2 Samuel 22:29

AUGUST 17

GOD'S APPLAUSE

It matters not if the world has heard
or approves or understands ...
The only applause we're meant to seek
is that of nail-scarred hands.

I know your deeds, your hard
work and your perseverance.
Revelation 2:2

AUGUST 18

WHATEVER I NEED

Lord, I know You will give me
whatever I need
that Your wise loving plan
for my life may succeed.

May the God of peace, equip you with
everything good for doing his will, and may
he work in us what is pleasing to him.
Hebrews 13:20-21

AUGUST 19

FIRST IN MY HEART

I will not find God upon the mountain
or in a vision or in nature's glory
until I find Him first in my heart.

Love the Lord your God with all
your heart and with all your soul and with
all your mind and with all your strength.

Mark 12:30

AUGUST 20

A STEP CLOSER

Lord, help me to look beyond my distress
and see Your love, so eager to bless.
Help me to see every trial I go through
as another step leading me closer to You.

*Consider it pure joy, my brothers, whenever you
face trials of many kinds, because you know that
the testing of your faith develops perseverance.*

James 1:2-3

AUGUST 21

CELEBRATION

In times of exultation,
in simple, quiet moments, too –
I live in celebration, Lord,
because I live in You.

*I will sing to the LORD all my life; I will
sing praise to my God as long as I live.*

Psalm 104:33

AUGUST 22

THE TRUTH OF HIS PROMISE

How vast and wondrous are the
heavens above the endless sea;
How beautiful the earth,
how grand the mountains' majesty;
How great, how true, the promise is
that He who made it all
Still clothes the lilies of the field
and heeds the sparrow's fall.

Yet not one of them will fall to the ground apart
from the will of your Father. So don't be afraid;
you are worth more than many sparrows.

Matthew 10:29, 31

AUGUST 23

ON THE MOUNTAINTOP

Here I stand, Lord,
in awe of Your goodness,
amazed by Your grace,
rejoicing in Your presence.
Here I stand ...
on the mountaintop with You.

He makes my feet like the feet of a deer;
he enables me to stand on the heights.

Psalm 18:33

AUGUST 24

THE LIGHT OF GOD'S LOVE

Only the light of God's love
can break through the shadows
of doubt and uncertainty ...
Only the light of God's love
can lead through life
to the gate of eternity.

The LORD is God, and he has
made his light shine upon us.

Psalm 118:27

AUGUST 25

A BLESSED PLACE

Any place with You, Lord,
is a blessed place.
Any time in Your presence
is a season of rejoicing.

*Hallelujah! For our Lord God
Almighty reigns. Let us rejoice
and be glad and give him glory!*
Revelation 19:6-7

AUGUST 26

REFLECTIONS OF HIS LOVE

Lord, make me daily aware
of the breathtaking beauty,
the glories of creation,
that so wondrously proclaim
Your awesome power,
yet so exquisitely and tenderly
reflect Your love.

The heavens declare the glory of God;
the skies proclaim the work of his hands.

Psalm 19:1

AUGUST 27

THE EVERLASTING LIGHT

He's our hope and consolation ...
He's our refuge in the night ...
He's our Friend and our salvation ...
Christ, the Everlasting Light.

Your sun will never set again,
and your moon will wane no more; the
LORD will be your everlasting light.
Isaiah 60:20

AUGUST 28

HEALING LOVE

The God who takes a summer storm
and ends it with a rainbow,
who lights the very darkest night
with silver stars above,
the God who, with a tiny seed,
can form a perfect rosebud,
is our God, and the One who heals
our heartaches with His love.

You removed my sackcloth and clothed me with joy,
that my heart may sing to you and not be silent.
O LORD my God, I will give you thanks forever.

Psalm 30:11-12

AUGUST 29

THE VERY LEAST OF US

The Lord who chose a shepherd boy
and made him king of Israel
can use the very least of us
to accomplish great things for Him.

*The LORD does not look at the things
man looks at. Man looks at the outward
appearance, but the LORD looks at the heart.*
1 Samuel 16:7

AUGUST 30

HERE I AM

The One we often look for in lofty places
stands among us, coming to meet us
at the place of our need.
In the midst of our failure,
our sin and our shame,
He is there with outstretched hands,
quietly waiting, gently saying,
"Here I am ... come as you are
... come to Me."

Before they call I will answer;
while they are still speaking I will hear.

Isaiah 65:24

AUGUST 31

NEVER ALONE

In the midst of the storm
comes a glimpse of a rainbow,
a banner of hope lifted over God's own.
We stand sheltered beneath it,
awaiting the sunshine,
assured by His Word
that we're never alone.

*You have been a refuge for the poor,
a refuge for the needy in his distress, a shelter
from the storm and a shade from the heat.*

Isaiah 25:4

September

SEPTEMBER 1

GOD'S WILL AND WISDOM

We ask for many things, Lord –
For peace and painless living,
solutions to our problems,
shelter, security, and safekeeping –
Teach us to value more Your will
and Your wisdom
than our own comfort and well-being.

*If any of you lacks wisdom, he should
ask God, who gives generously to all.*
James 1:5

SEPTEMBER 2

THE SHELTER OF HIS LOVE

His presence is a fortress
with walls that never fall ...
He hides us in the shelter of His love.

Praise be to the LORD, for he
showed his wonderful love to me.

Psalm 31:21

SEPTEMBER 3

HOW GREAT IS YOUR LOVE

Make us aware of Your longing heart, Lord –
Let us not be too blind to see
How far You will go, how great is Your love –
Remind us of Calvary.

Greater love has no one than this,
that he lay down his life for his friends.
John 15:13

SEPTEMBER 4

TO GLORIFY YOU

Loving Lord ...
Let me never forget
in whatever I do
that the goal of my life
is to glorify You.

*Whatever you do, work at it with all
your heart, as working for the Lord, not
for men, since you know that you will receive
an inheritance from the Lord as a reward.*

Colossians 3:23-24

SEPTEMBER 5

A GRAND ADVENTURE

God's intent for us
is never anchored in tomorrow –
His purpose is for here and now ... today.
God wants this life to be a grand adventure,
not a blueprint.
Our part is to trust Him and obey.

Whoever gives heed to instruction prospers,
and blessed is he who trusts in the Lord.
Proverbs 16:20

SEPTEMBER 6

ASSURED OF VICTORY

Centered in the Divine Constancy,
protected by Divine Care,
we face life's trials assured of victory.

We are hard pressed on every side, but not crushed;
perplexed, but not in despair; persecuted, but
not abandoned; struck down, but not destroyed.

2 Corinthians 4:8-9

ANOTHER DREAM

Hold fast your dreams and live your life
with hope that every day
will bring, with every dream come true,
another dream your way.

But hope that is seen is no hope at all.
Who hopes for what he already has?

Romans 8:24

SEPTEMBER 8

HOPE AND ASSURANCE

We have a God who seems to delight
in doing impossible things –
When we're at the end of our strength,
He's only begun.
We can face every trial
without fear of defeat,
for this is our hope and assurance:
With God at our side the battle is already won.

Delight yourself in the LORD and he
will give you the desires of your heart.

Psalm 37:4

SEPTEMBER 9

ONE STOP

We glorify God best
by taking one step at a time;
We please Him most by living every hour
in constant celebration
of His never-failing love
and in absolute dependence on His power.

I will praise you, O Lord my God, with
all my heart; I will glorify your name forever.
Psalm 86:12

SEPTEMBER 10

ONLY GOOD

Lord, guide my thoughts
and guard my words that only good
will escape my lips.

*May the words of my mouth and the
meditation of my heart be pleasing in your
sight, O LORD, my Rock and my Redeemer.*

Psalm 19:14

SEPTEMBER 11

THE GLORY OF YOUR LOVE

This is my mountaintop,
my place of celebration –
not in a work of wonder
or on a pinnacle of power –
but here, in this ordinary place,
where the only mystery
is the heartbeat of my life,
and where the only wonders
are the commonplace things
touched by the glory of Your love.

O LORD my God, I will give you thanks forever.

Psalm 30:12

SEPTEMBER 12

PREVAILING GOODNESS

Hope may falter for a time,
strength and help may fail,
but through it all the Lord stands by –
His goodness will prevail.

I will sing of your strength, in the morning
I will sing of your love; for you are my
fortress, my refuge in times of trouble.
Psalm 59:16

SEPTEMBER 13

A FAITH TO FOLLOW

Thank You, Lord,
for every season of the soul ...
For giving us a faith to follow,
a hope to cling to,
a promise to sustain us
as we journey toward
our eternal tomorrow with You.

*Therefore we do not lose heart. For our light and
momentary troubles are achieving for us an eternal
glory that far outweighs them all. So we fix our
eyes not on what is seen, but on what is unseen.*

2 Corinthians 4:16-18

SEPTEMBER 14

HAND-IN-HAND

We fulfil God's purpose
And delight His heart as well
When we walk the journey
with Him, hand-in-hand.
We discover that His presence
Makes every moment something precious
when we're living the adventure
that He planned.

Show me your ways, O LORD, teach me your
paths; guide me in your truth and teach me.

Psalm 25:45

SEPTEMBER 15

HOLY THINGS

A quilt of wildflowers on a field,
an autumn anthem lifted
by wild geese on the wing,
a frost-laced grove
of tall pines at early morning ...
in our Creator-God's eyes,
are these not holy things,
as sacred as stained glass and altars?

*God saw all that he had made,
and it was very good.*
Genesis 1:31

SEPTEMBER 16

RESTORED DREAMS

He invites us to bring
our worn, frayed hopes,
our broken dreams, our care-laden hearts
and let Him relieve and restore and renew
as we rest in His love.

*You prepare a table before me in the
presence of my enemies. You anoint
my head with oil; my cup overflows.*

Psalm 23:5

September 17

God Comes

The glory of God is not always found
in the mystic or the fantastic
or in times of exultation ...
More often God reveals His presence
in gentle ways. In a quiet moment at dawn,
in the sighing of the wind,
in the whisper of a prayer ...
God comes.

He makes me lie down in green pastures, he leads
me beside quiet waters, he restores my soul.

Psalm 23:2

SEPTEMBER 18

YOUR BLESSED NAME

Just the speaking of Your blessed name
brings peace and comfort ...
My soul loves the very sound of JESUS.

*You came near when I called
you, and you said, "Do not fear."*
Lamentations 3:57

SEPTEMBER 19

CLOSE TO HIS HEART

My Shepherd carries me
close to His heart when I hurt ...
In the warmth of His love,
I am healed and made whole.

I am the good shepherd; I know
my sheep and my sheep know me
and I lay down my life for the sheep.
John 10:14-15

SEPTEMBER 20

LIVE IN GOD'S LOVE

Hope is the light that makes us reach higher
And bids us aspire to be all we can be.
Faith is the wind that lifts us above
To live in God's love, joyfully free.

*Therefore, since we have been justified
through faith, we have peace with God
through our Lord Jesus Christ. And
we rejoice in the hope of the glory of God.*

Romans 5:1-2

SEPTEMBER 21

GREATER LOVE

Too many times, Lord,
when I see a dream die,
I lose hope because my plans
have come to nothing.
Help me to remember
that Your love is always
greater than my disappointments ...
and Your plan for my life
is always better than my brightest dreams.

*Pray that the eyes of your heart may be enlightened that
you may know the hope to which he has called you.*

Ephesians 1:18

SEPTEMBER 22

A HEART OF WONDER

Give me a heart of wonder, Lord ...
Let me always see the splendor
in a patch of wildflowers,
sense the mystery of a fog-curtained
river at dawn,
admire the grace of a country lane,
and celebrate the glory of a rainbow.

O LORD my God, you are very great;
you are clothed with splendor and majesty.
He wraps himself in light as with a garment;
he stretches out the heavens like a tent.

Psalm 104:1-3

SEPTEMBER 23

EYES OF HOPE

Look at the world through eyes of hope –
see every day as a promise.
Search for the beautiful, seek out life's best,
follow the path of the rainbow.

*Let us hold unswervingly to the hope we
profess, for he who promised is faithful.*
Hebrews 10:23

SEPTEMBER 24

GOODNESS AND MERCY

Lord, help me to stand firm in Your will,
knowing I also stand sheltered in Your love.
Throughout each trial,
beyond every struggle, there is Your mercy,
Your comfort and Your goodness.

You have heard of Job's perseverance and
have seen what the Lord finally brought about.
The Lord is full of compassion and mercy.

James 5:11

SEPTEMBER 25

THE RAIN OF HIS SPIRIT

Thank Him for the storms
that break open the dry, parched ground
and allow the renewing rain of His Spirit
to pour into our lives ...
It's the weight of the wind
and the force of the storm
that make deep, sturdy roots
and strong solid trees.

*Blessed is the man who trusts in the LORD, whose
confidence is in him. He will be like a tree planted by
the water that sends out its roots by the stream.*

Jeremiah 17:7-8

SEPTEMBER 26

FAITH WITH WINGS

The Father's own assurance
that He's with us in all things
gives us courage and endurance
and provides our faith with wings.

I am with you and will watch over you
wherever you go. I will not leave you until
I have done what I have promised you.

Genesis 28:15

SEPTEMBER 27

THE ONLY GOD

My strength at all times and in all things
is the assurance that my God
is the God who creates,
the God who saves,
the God who heals,
the only God,
the one God who never fails.

Be strong and courageous. Do not be afraid
for the LORD your God goes with you; he
will never leave you nor forsake you.

Deuteronomy 31:6

SEPTEMBER 28

THE WAY OF THE CROSS

God's Word makes it clear
that the way of the cross
will sometimes bring sacrifice,
suffering and loss.
But He promises also
to walk at our side
as our Light for the journey,
our Friend and our Guide.

Whoever finds his life will lose it, and
whoever loses his life for my sake will find it.
Matthew 10:39

September 29

Renew My Hope

Your presence gladdens my heart, Lord;
Your promises renew my hope.
Never have You delayed Your deliverance
beyond the right time, the best time,
to display Your power.

"Because he loves me," says the LORD,
"I will rescue him; I will be with him in
trouble, I will deliver him and honor him."
Psalm 91:14-15

SEPTEMBER 30

HELP ME STAND

Lord, when weakness seems to be
the very essence of my days,
remind me of Your promises –
and help me stand ...
In the power of Your Word,
in the quiet of Your Peace,
in the light of Your love –
help me stand.

*If you make the Most High your
dwelling then no harm will befall you.*
Psalm 91:9-10

October

OCTOBER 1

REJOICE IN THIS

This truth makes my soul rejoice,
my spirit sing ...
that today, in this hour,
I am in the presence of the King.

*In the presence of the LORD your
God, you shall eat and shall rejoice in
everything you have put your hand to, because
the LORD your God has blessed you.*

Deuteronomy 12:7

OCTOBER 2

WALK IN FAITH

Help me to remember
Your past faithfulness –
the countless times You've led me
through the shadows
or carried me above a storm
to set me in a safe place –
Help me to walk in faith,
depending on You.

I guide you in the way of wisdom and lead you along
straight paths. When you walk, your steps will not
be hampered; when you run, you will not stumble.

Proverbs 4:11-12

OCTOBER 3

A LIFE PLEASING TO YOU

Lord, enable me to live
a joyful, prayerful, thankful life –
A life that is pleasing to You.

Be joyful always; pray continually;
give thanks in all circumstances, for this
is God's will for you in Christ Jesus.

1 Thessalonians 5:16-18

OCTOBER 4

THE QUIET HEART

The quiet heart finds blessing
in small gifts of gentle beauty,
assurance in warm, peaceful hours of rest.
The quiet heart finds joy
and true contentment always nearby,
for the quiet heart knows
simple things are best.

Godliness with contentment is great gain.

1 Timothy 6:6

OCTOBER 5

WITH ALL HIS HEART

Let me be like David, Lord,
who through all his successes and defeats,
his triumphs and failures,
among the monuments
and amid the ruins of his life –
loved You with all his heart.

My heart is steadfast, O God; I will
sing and make music with all my soul.
Psalm 108:1

OCTOBER 6

JESUS IS HIS NAME

He is the *hope* for all the hopeless,
The *way* for those who seek,
A *light* for those in darkness,
A *helper* for the weak,
He is *freedom* for the prisoner,
A *ransom* for our shame,
He is *Savior*, *Lord*, and *Master* –
And *Jesus* is His name.

At the name of Jesus every knee should bow,
and every tongue confess that Jesus Christ is
Lord, to the glory of God the Father.

Philippians 2:10-11

OCTOBER 7

CONSTANT LOVE

His love is as constant
in the darkness as in the light,
as faithful in the silence
as amidst the sounds of singing ...
In His time, He comes to rescue and restore
all those who wait for Him.

The LORD, the LORD, the compassionate
and gracious God, slow to anger,
abounding in love and faithfulness.

Exodus 34:6

OCTOBER 8

A TIME OF STILL WATERS

There's a time of still waters
that comes to us all,
a time when we hear
the Lord's soft, gentle call ...
He asks us to trust Him
to be still and rest,
as He works to accomplish
His will for our best.

*There is a river whose streams
make glad the city of God, the holy
place where the Most High dwells.*

Psalm 46:4

OCTOBER 9

SUNSHINE THOUGHTS

Set your heart on brighter things –
Each day contains a promise.
Light the hours with sunshine thoughts
And hope will paint a rainbow.

*Command those who are rich in this
present world not to put their hope in wealth
but to put their hope in God, who richly
provides us with everything for our enjoyment.*
1 Timothy 6:17

OCTOBER 10

BECAUSE OF THE CROSS

Because of the Cross,
my past is forgiven,
my future assured ...
Because of the Cross,
I can live today
fully and freely with hope.

He forgave us all our sins, having canceled
the written code, with its regulations, that
was against us and that stood opposed to
us; he took it away, nailing it to the cross.

Colossians 2:13-14

OCTOBER 11

BEING STILL

He calls us out of the crowd and clamor,
away from the noise of getting things done,
accomplishing goals and achieving,
away from reaching and striving,
into the quiet and peace of just ... being.
In the simple act of being still and trusting,
we finally fulfil His will.

Make it your ambition to lead a quiet life.

1 Thessalonians 4:11

OCTOBER 12

IN YOU

Lord, let me never forget
that I can do all things in You
and nothing without You.

Jesus looked at them and said,
"With man this is impossible, but
with God all things are possible."
Matthew 19:26

OCTOBER 13

HIS LOVE SHINES ON

His love shines on ...
beyond time's distant, vast horizon,
past yesterday, today, and each tomorrow ...
though joy grows dim
and sunlight fades to shadow,
His love shines on,
within our hearts,
beyond our sorrow.

*Even the darkness will not be
dark to you; the night will shine like
the day, for darkness is as light to you.*

Psalm 139:12

OCTOBER 14

HOPE

Hope reaches out to life
with faith and glad anticipation ...
Hope steps out, free of doubt,
to live in celebration.

*I will praise you forever for what
you have done; in your name I
will hope, for your name is good.*

Psalm 52:9

OCTOBER 15

THE BEAUTY OF LIFE

Oh, Lord, You have taught me
that my life is changed
only by meeting You,
that my life has meaning and value
and beauty only when
fully surrendered to You.

The Lord has anointed me to bestow on
[those who grieve] a crown of beauty instead of
ashes, the oil of gladness instead of mourning, and
a garment of praise instead of a spirit of despair.

Isaiah 61:1, 3

OCTOBER 16

THE POWER OF YOUR WORD

Lord, let my peace be founded
on nothing less
than the power of Your Word.

*I will listen to what God the L*ORD
will say; he promises peace to his people.

Psalm 85:8

OCTOBER 17

WHISPERED WORDS

In the quiet You have so often
whispered words of comfort ...
In the silent waiting of my soul,
You have confirmed Your love.

You have given me comfort and
have spoken kindly to your servant.

Ruth 2:13

OCTOBER 18

TRUST HIS LOVE

Trust His will ... the Lord is faithful
and He only wants our best.
Trust His Word ... within its promises
His goodness is expressed.
Trust His power ... He is Almighty,
the Creator of all things.
Trust His love ... we are His family,
children of the King of kings.

*Trust in the LORD with all your heart
and lean not on your own understanding.*

Proverbs 3:5

OCTOBER 19

THE PRAYERS OF MY HEART

Lord, teach me how
to align my prayer to Your loving will,
to come to You
with the unshakeable confidence
that the prayers of my heart
reach Your ear.

This is the confidence we have in
approaching God: that if we ask anything
according to his will, he hears us.

1 John 5:14

OCTOBER 20

ETERNAL LOVE

He has always loved us,
even before the Cross ...
It was love that sent Him there,
love that held Him there,
love that draws us there.

This is love: not that we loved God,
but that he loved us and sent his Son
as an atoning sacrifice for our sins.

1 John 4:10

OCTOBER 21

WHAT I AM

Remind me often, Lord,
that You are more interested
in what I am
than in what I do.

For it is by grace you have been saved, through
faith – and this not from yourselves, it is the gift
of God – not by works, so that no one can boast.

Ephesians 2:8-9

OCTOBER 26

THE GIFT OF PRAYER

Prayer is a many-faceted gift,
a gift that goes on giving,
the only gift that can make a real difference
in the life of someone we love.

I thank my God every time I remember you. In all
my prayers for all of you, I always pray with joy.
Philippians 1:3-4

OCTOBER 27

GOD IS FAITHFUL

In the midst of our failure and weakness,
God is faithful
and able to forgive and restore.

Do not be afraid or discouraged, for
the LORD God, my God, is with you.
He will not fail you or forsake you.

1 Chronicles 28:20

OCTOBER 28

GOD DELIGHTS IN US

God comforts us
in the valley of our despair ...
He rejoices with us
on the heights of our celebration ...
And through it all, He delights
in our unfaltering faith and praise.

*I will turn their mourning into gladness; I will
give them comfort and joy instead of sorrow.*
Jeremiah 31:13

OCTOBER 29

SEEK HIS PATH

I come before You, Jesus,
weak but willing ...
I seek to walk Your path,
and not my own.

If the LORD delights in a man's way, he makes
his steps firm; though he stumble, he will not
fall, for the LORD upholds him with his hand.
Psalm 37:23-24 –

OCTOBER 30

ORDINARY PEOPLE

God never chooses His workers
based on wealth or fame or social status.
He calls out ordinary people
to accomplish extraordinary things,
enabled and empowered by His Spirit.

*There are different kinds of gifts, but the same
Spirit. There are different kinds of service, but the
same Lord. There are different kinds of working,
but the same God works all of them in all men.*

1 Corinthians 12:4-6

OCTOBER 31

BLESSED ASSURANCE

Lord of All Peace,
Blessed Assurance ...
Your Presence gladdens my heart,
Your Promises renew my hope ...
Your Power strengthens my desire
to seek Your will and quickly obey.

*May you be richly rewarded by the
Lord, the God of Israel, under whose
wings you have come to take refuge.*

Ruth 2:12

November

NOVEMBER 1

LAMB OF GOD

Suffering Savior, Lamb of God ...
thank You for Your sacrificial love ...
For standing in for me at Calvary,
taking my place, erasing my sin,
redeeming my soul.

He was pierced for our transgressions, he
was crushed for our iniquities; the
punishment that brought us peace was upon
him, and by his wounds we are healed.

Isaiah 53:5

NOVEMBER 2

MOLD US

Only our suffering Savior
can use times of pain and loneliness
to mold us in wisdom and faithfulness.

*We know that in all things God works for
the good of those who love him, who
have been called according to his purpose.*

Romans 8:28

NOVEMBER 3

THE WINDOW OF LIFE

Lord, help me to look at life
through a window, not a mirror.

*Each of you should look not only to your own
interests, but also to the interests of others. Your
attitude should be the same as that of Christ Jesus.*

Philippians 2:4-5

NOVEMBER 4

AN ANTHEM OF PRAISE

When the winter of my years
has come upon me, Lord,
may I still sing an anthem of praise
for every springtime beauty given,
every rose of summer savored,
every autumn harvest gathered in
from Your generous hands of love.

I will bless them and the places surrounding
my hill. I will send down showers in
season; there will be showers of blessing.
Ezekiel 34:26

November 5

Guide My Steps

Lord, guide my steps along life's journey;
Hold my hand along the way.
Point me in the right direction
As I travel day by day.

*Show me your ways, O Lord, teach me your
paths; guide me in your truth and teach me.*

Psalm 25:4-5

NOVEMBER 6

A WALK OF FAITH

Keep me mindful of Your presence
When the shadows hide my view;
Make my life in every season
A daily walk of faith with You.

*Remember, O LORD, how I have walked
before you faithfully and with wholehearted
devotion and have done what is good in your eyes.*
2 Kings 20:3

November 7

Serenity

Lord, grant us tranquility in storm or strife,
serenity in all of life,
that when You whisper, "Peace, be still,"
we'll wait upon Your perfect will,
knowing we will soon be blessed
by Love that only wants our best.

Submit to God and be at peace with him;
in this way prosperity will come to you.
Job 22:21

NOVEMBER 8

GREAT PATIENCE

Lord, help me to remember
that You are not confined
or restricted by Time.
I can only see Today, but You see
Yesterday, Tomorrow and Eternity ...
Teach me a great patience,
a patience founded
on the One who was and is and ever will be.

*With the Lord a day is like a thousand
years, and a thousand years are like a day.*
2 Peter 3:8

NOVEMBER 9

TO GLORIFY YOU

If my work seems too small,
Let me quickly recall
That I do what I do
That the world may know You.

Whatever you do, whether in word or deed,
do it all in the name of the Lord Jesus,
giving thanks to God the Father through him.
Colossians 3:17

NOVEMBER 10

THE LOVE OF THE FATHER

Father of Love ...
Help me to make the choice
to love others,
just as You chose to love me.

Dear friends, since God so loved us,
we also ought to love one another.

1 John 4:11

November 11

Eternal spring

Our God, Lord of all life's changing seasons,
Lord of everything that's been
and that will be,
has promised us,
when winter's finally over,
an endless spring in His eternity.

*Surely you have granted him eternal blessings and
made him glad with the joy of your presence.*

Psalm 21:6

NOVEMBER 12

GOD'S LOVE AND GOODNESS

For the steadfast love
and goodness of the Lord
who reigns forever,
I will sing Alleluia in my heart.

*I will sing of the LORD's great
love forever; with my mouth I will make
your faithfulness known through all generations.*

Psalm 89:1

NOVEMBER 13

YOUR PRESENCE

In this quiet hour, Lord,
come to bless me ...
Let me know nothing but
Your presence and Your peace.

*Is not the LORD your God with you? And
has he not granted you rest on every side?*

1 Chronicles 22:18

348

NOVEMBER 14

THE RHYTHM OF LIFE

Let me live in harmony
with the Creator and His created.
Let me live a life in which love
gives the rhythm to every season,
a life whose winter is an Alleluia –
a triumphant overture to Eternal Spring.

Live in harmony with one another; be sympathetic,
love as brothers, be compassionate and humble.

1 Peter 3:8

NOVEMBER 15

A PROMISE OF GOD

I have learned at last
that suffering at its worst
can never outlast a promise of God,
never outlive His love.

Weeping may remain for a night,
but rejoicing comes in the morning.

Psalm 30:5

NOVEMBER 16

A HARVEST OF BLESSING

Lord, let my life bear fruit that,
even when I'm gone,
will bring a harvest of blessing
and goodness to others.

*I am the vine; you are the branches. If a
man remains in me and I in him, he will bear
much fruit; apart from me you can do nothing.*

John 15:5

NOVEMBER 17

AN OFFERING OF PRAISE

Lord, make my life, day by day,
a song of thanksgiving,
an offering of praise,
a celebration of Your love
and Your amazing grace.

Through Jesus, therefore, let us continually
offer to God a sacrifice of praise – the
fruit of lips that confess his name.

Hebrews 13:15

NOVEMBER 18

HE IS GOD

He is faithful ...
Steadfast ...
Ever-present ...
Never-changing ...
Ancient and eternal ...
He is God.

Know therefore that the LORD your God is God; he is the faithful God, keeping his covenant of love to a thousand generations of those who love him and keep his commands.

Deuteronomy 7:9

NOVEMBER 19

EACH DAY

Let me live a life each day
that will honor Your name
and delight Your heart.

He did what was right and just,
so all went well with him.

Jeremiah 22:15

NOVEMBER 20

UNEXPECTED GRACE

God gives us grace
for all our days,
in small and unexpected ways,
to bless the heart
and lift the spirit skyward.

And I will pour out on the house of David and
the inhabitants of Jerusalem a spirit of grace.

Zechariah 12:10

NOVEMBER 21

GOD BE THANKED

God be thanked ...
For precious times of peace
and warm contentment,
For moments that make memories
we can hold forever near,
For priceless gifts of love
and gentle blessings,
For joy that goes on shining
in the heart from year to year.

*Give thanks to the LORD, call on his name; Sing to
him, sing praise to him; tell of all his wonderful acts.*

1 Chronicles 16:8-9

NOVEMBER 22

SIMPLE THINGS

God, help us to rejoice in simple things –
the work You've given us to do,
the health and strength with which to do it ...
the food You've given us to eat,
the family gathered close to share it ...
the gift of another day to live,
and the grace and goodness to enjoy it.

*The LORD has done this, and
it is marvelous in our eyes.*

Psalm 118:23

November 23

Blessings of Joy

I will quiet my heart and
rest in His presence –
The Lord longs to heal and restore me.
I'll take strength from His love
and find hope in believing
new blessings of joy lie before me.

He will cover you with his feathers,
and under his wings you will find refuge.

Psalm 91:4

NOVEMBER 24

WE ARE BLESSED

For strength to work, for joy to sing,
For faith's bright hope and freedom's dream,
For harvest time and days of rest,
We give You thanks ... for we are blessed.

Great is the LORD and most worthy of
praise; his greatness no one can fathom.

Psalm 145:3

November 25

Love One Another

What can we give Him for all that He's done?
He has given us everything – even His Son.
Perhaps if we asked Him how best
to convey our thanksgiving, He'd smile,
and then quietly say, "There's but
one thing I ask all my children to do:
Love one another as I have loved you."

*Dear children, let us not love with words
or tongue but with actions and in truth.*

1 John 3:18

November 26

Thankful hearts

Lord, enable us to live
With thankful hearts at every moment,
Mindful of our blessings, big and small.
May we never take for granted
Your abundant gifts of goodness,
But continually be grateful for them all.

Devote yourselves to prayer,
being watchful and thankful.
Colossians 4:2

NOVEMBER 27

FOR TODAY

God is guiding me and training me
for today – not for someday.
His purpose for my life
is in the present moment,
here and now.

As long as it is day, we must do
the work of him who sent me.

John 9:4

NOVEMBER 28

YOUR DIRECTION

Lord, remind me to take time
to study the map
before racing down the road,
to look for signposts
and wait for Your direction
as I travel on the way.

*It is not good to have zeal without
knowledge, nor to be hasty and miss the way.*

Proverbs 19:2

NOVEMBER 29

EXPLORE YOUR WORD

Father, give us a hunger to explore
Your Word, to discover the truth
that will change our lives
and enrich the lives of others.

*For the word of God is living and active. Sharper
than any double-edged sword, it penetrates even
to dividing soul and spirit, joints and marrow; it
judges the thoughts and attitudes of the heart.*

Hebrews 4:12

November 30

God's every promise

God has pledged to us a love
we can't begin to comprehend,
A love fulfilled and sealed by sacrifice.
He sent His only Son
as confirmation of that love –
God's every promise finds
its "Yes" in Christ.

For no matter how many promises
God has made, they are "Yes" in Christ.
2 Corinthians 1:20

December

DECEMBER 1

TO WELCOME YOU

Gentle Savior,
Give me a quiet heart,
always open to Your coming,
ever sensitive to Your whisper,
quick and eager to welcome You
with gladness and rejoicing.

The unfading beauty of a gentle and quiet
spirit is of great worth in God's sight.
1 Peter 3:4

DECEMBER 2

CHERISHED BLESSINGS

Keep a place, a quiet place,
for all your little joys,
those cherished blessings
gathered year to year ...
A place where all the lovely things,
the very best and brightest things,
will always wait to warm your heart with cheer.

The house of the righteous contains great treasure.

Proverbs 15:6

DECEMBER 3

THE WONDROUS NAME OF JESUS

At Your name, Lord –
Your precious name –
My heart bows, my soul exults,
my spirit rejoices.
May all that I am,
all that You created me to be,
celebrate the wondrous name of JESUS.

On his robe and on his thigh he has this name
written: KING OF KINGS AND LORD OF LORDS.
Revelation 19:16

DECEMBER 4

THE LIGHT OF HIS LOVE

We can take the troubles we daily bear
and place them in God's loving care,
for His desire is to set us free
from worry, fear and anxiety ...
Our burden gone, we then look above,
past every storm, to the light of His love.

Cast your cares on the LORD
and he will sustain you.

Psalm 55:22

DECEMBER 5

THE LASTING GIFT

God's Love ...
The one lasting gift of perfection –
A wonder, a glory, the truest reflection
of His caring heart for the world He created –
God's love is a gift meant to be celebrated.

*How great is the love the Father
has lavished on us, that we should
be called children of God!*

1 John 3:1

DECEMBER 6

SO GENTLE A NAME

Jesus ...
A name to subdue
mighty oceans and nations,
A name to tame
hurricane winds and wild beasts,
A name to call forth praise
from all God's creation,
yet so gentle a name
that we call Him our Peace.

He himself is our peace.
Ephesians 2:14

DECEMBER 7

HEAVEN'S DOOR

Christ was born to deliver His people ...
He lived to unlock heaven's door ...
He died to redeem His creation ...
He lives, King of kings, evermore.

Christ died and returned to life
so that he might be the Lord of both
the dead and the living.

Romans 14:9

DECEMBER 8

HIS QUIET COMING

His coming was quiet ...
no clash of cymbals, no blast of trumpets ...
just the midnight song of angels
and the awe-filled sighs of shepherds
on a hillside hushed by holiness.
His coming is still quiet ...
Just a whisper of love in the silence
and a gentle promise to the humble heart
that bids Him welcome.

If my people, who are called by my name, will humble
themselves and pray, then will I hear from heaven.

2 Chronicles 7:14

DECEMBER 9

BLESSING OF TRANQUILITY

Lord, teach me true serenity,
the blessing of tranquillity.
Let me find my deepest joy in Thee –
Give me peace within Your love.

*Better one handful with tranquillity than two
handfuls with toil and chasing after the wind.*

Ecclesiastes 4:6

DECEMBER 10

ABUNDANT LIFE

Jesus ...
The fullness of the Father's love
is contained in Your blessed name.
May my life every day reflect that love
and draw others to the abundant life in You.

*She will give birth to a son, and you
are to give him the name Jesus, because he
will save his people from their sins.*

Matthew 1:21

December 11

Grace and goodness

There is no darkness in the heart
where Your love lives, Lord ...
No shadows dimming the horizon
of Today or days to come.
Your grace and goodness, ever new,
bring light and hope to all of life ...
Lord, shine Your love into my heart
today and always.

The star they had seen in the east
went ahead of them until it stopped
over the place where the child was.

Matthew 2:9

DECEMBER 12

HOPE AND GLORY

Messiah ...
The majesty of God
in the humility of a Child ...
Glory in a manger-bed,
Hope in an infant's sigh.

We have found the Messiah (that is, the Christ).
John 1:41

DECEMBER 13

THE TIME OF YOUR COMING

I kneel before You, Lord,
asking You to open my heart
and prepare my spirit for Your indwelling
as the time of Your coming draws near.

Here I am! I stand at the door and knock.
If anyone hears my voice and opens the door,
I will come in and eat with him, and he with me.
Revelation 3:20

DECEMBER 14

THE LIGHT OF EVERY HEART

His love is the bright and shining star
of every season ...
His love is the light and life
of every heart that welcomes Him.

I am the light of the world.

John 8:12

DECEMBER 15

HOPE IN OUR HEARTS

Let us come to the season
with hope in our hearts ...
Let us gather together and bring
a new prayer for peace
and goodwill toward all people
as gifts for our Savior and King.

Then they opened their treasures
and presented him with gifts of
gold and of incense and of myrrh.
Matthew 2:11

DECEMBER 16

TO HUMBLE HEARTS

Gently comes the Prince of Peace,
The King of all creation;
To humble hearts His love imparts
The gift of God's salvation.

The gift of God is eternal life
in Christ Jesus our Lord.
Romans 6:23

DECEMBER 17

GOD CAME

God spoke ...
and Light broke through the darkness.
God came ...
and Love broke through the light.
God be praised ...
for the Light and the Love of Jesus.

The light shines in the darkness.

John 1:5

DECEMBER 18

A GENTLE CHRISTMAS

Cherish the wonder, the peace,
of a gentle Christmas ...
Let the holy hush of the Judaen hills
enfold your heart and touch the season
with abiding joy.
Remember Bethlehem,
welcome the Savior,
and share His love.

*I bring you good news of great
joy that will be for all the people.*

Luke 2:10

DECEMBER 19

CHRIST OUR PEACE

Peace must be more than a word
embossed upon our Christmas cards,
echoed in the season's carols,
or painted on a storefront ...
It can be found only in a Person,
experienced only in a Presence ...
For Christ, and Christ alone is our Peace.

Glory to God in the highest, and on earth
peace to men on whom his favor rests.

Luke 2:14

DECEMBER 20

IN BETHLEHEM

One night in Bethlehem,
beneath a singing sky,
a royal Prince gave up His throne ...
a Shepherd came to seek His own ...
The Savior of the world was born
one night in Bethlehem.

*Today in the town of David a Savior has
been born to you; he is Christ the Lord.*

Luke 2:11

DECEMBER 21

A TINY BABE

Who would have thought He'd trade a throne
for swaddling and a manger,
appearing to the world He made
as just a tiny Stranger?
Who would have thought this tiny,
humble Babe would one day be
the King we'd praise, adore
and serve for all eternity?

*When the time had fully
come, God sent his Son.*
Galatians 4:4

DECEMBER 22

THE LASTING GIFTS

Lord, lift our eyes above
the trimmings and the tinsel ...
Let us look past temporary things
to see the lasting gifts
which You have promised,
the joy and peace
that life in Jesus brings.

Every good and perfect gift is from above.

James 1:17

DECEMBER 23

CHRISTMAS ...

Hymns have tried to capture all its wonder;
Books of wisdom leave it unexplained.
Paintings have attempted to portray it,
But its meaning will forever be contained
In the words a mother whispered by a manger,
A word she heard God's angel first proclaim:
JESUS ... all the shining glory of Christmas
Is found within that holy, precious name.

Therefore God exalted him to the highest place and
gave him the name that is above every name.
Philippians 2:9

DECEMBER 24

BEAUTY AND PEACE

Let us cherish this time of beauty and peace,
and keep it set apart
as a holy time of hope and love –
a season of the heart.

*Mary treasured up all these things
and pondered them in her heart.*

Luke 2:19

DECEMBER 25

KING OF ALL KINGS

JESUS ... the angels in heaven proclaim
the glory of God in one wonderful name ...
Announced by a star as the universe sings,
He comes as our Savior and King of all kings!

*You will be with child and give birth to a
son, and you are to give him the name Jesus.*
Luke 1:31

DECEMBER 26

HE HAS COME

Jesus the Christ ...
Proclaimed by prophets,
acclaimed by angels,
He has come, just as foretold.
Beloved Son, Anointed One,
in Him, God's glory is revealed.

The virgin will be with child and will give
birth to a son, and will call him Immanuel.

Isaiah 7:14

DECEMBER 27

IN HIM

In His birth is all hope ...
In His way is all light ...
In His Word is all truth ...
In His love is all life.

I am the way and the truth and the life.

John 14:6

DECEMBER 28

MY GUIDING HAND

God be in my life every
moment, every day ...
Be the guiding hand of everything I do.
Be my hope and aspiration,
Be my joy and inspiration,
Let each part of life,
the heart of life, be You.

O God, you are my God, earnestly I seek you;
my soul thirsts for you. Because your love is
better than life, my lips will glorify you. My soul
will be satisfied as with the richest of foods.

Psalm 63:1, 3, 5

DECEMBER 29

ANTHEM OF REJOICING

Make my life a melody
in tune with all creation –
Help me live in harmony
with every living thing.
Let my whole existence
be an anthem of rejoicing,
a prelude to eternal life with You,
my Lord and King.

*My heart leaps for joy and I
will give thanks to him in song.*
Psalm 28:7

DECEMBER 30

I'LL TRUST YOU STILL

I see Your hand, Lord,
in everythng around me,
and in every aspect of my life,
I seek Your will ...
I see Your plan, Lord,
in all the years behind me,
and in the days and years to come,
I'll trust You still.

The LORD gives strength to his people;
the LORD blesses his people with peace.

Psalm 29:11

DECEMBER 31

THE FOOTPRINTS OF HIS LOVE

Unknown, but not uncharted,
tomorrow waits for our arrival –
a day designed, a place prepared
with tender care by the One
who goes before us ...
Let us walk with faith behind Him
in the footprints of His love.

*Your word is a lamp to my
feet and a light for my path.*
Psalm 119:105